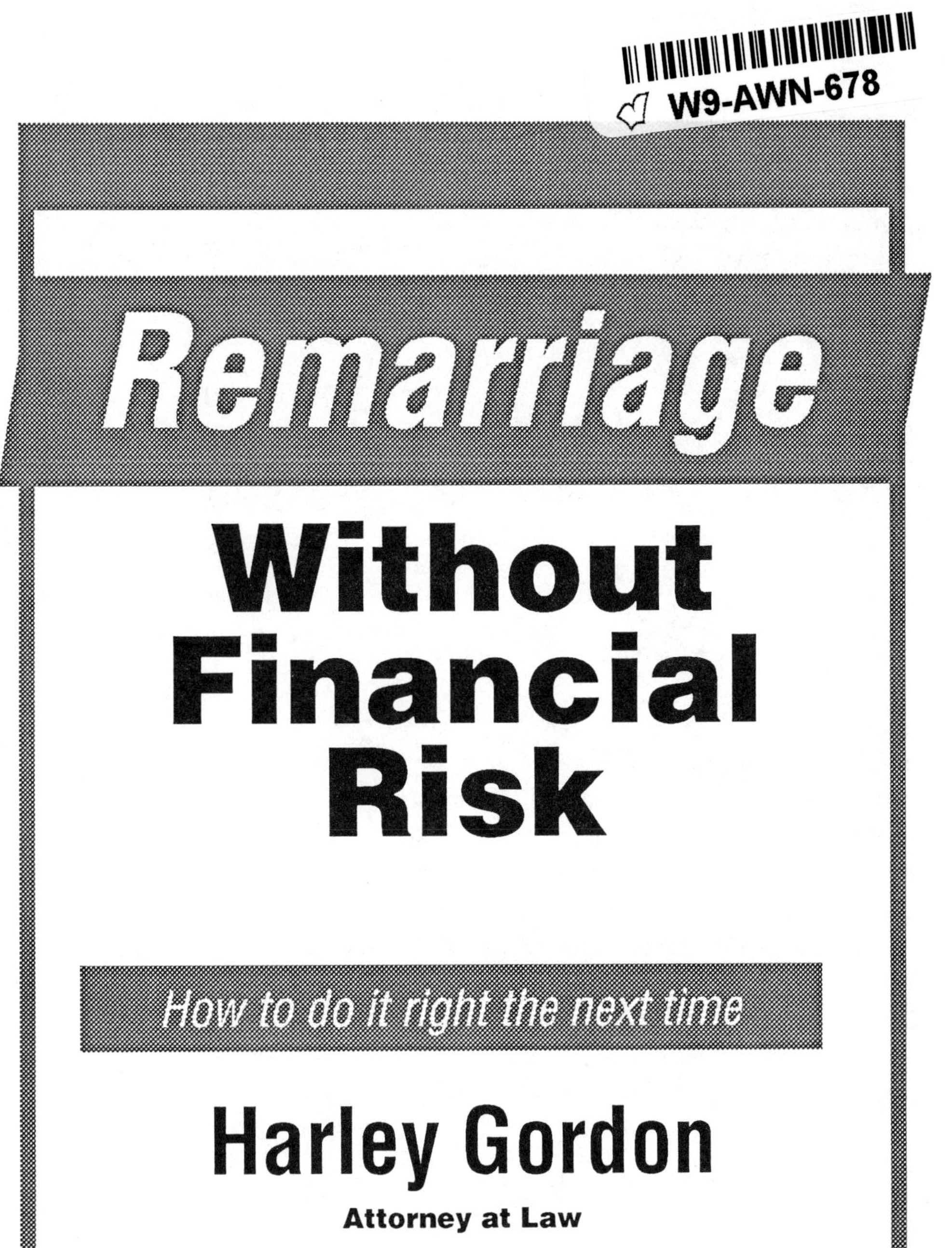

Harley Gordon
Attorney at Law
with
Jane Daniel

First Edition Published 1992

Designed by:
BECK *designs*
Debra Beck

Printed in the United States of America

ISBN 0-9625667-3-X
Library of Congress Catalog Card Number 92-74026

Financial Planning Institute, Inc.
P.O. Box 135
Boston, MA 02258
(617) 965-8120

Acknowledgements

SOME OF THE BEST MINDS in the business of law, finance and marital relations contributed their knowledge and experience to the writing of this book. The authors are indebted to them for giving us the opportunity to partake of their wisdom and to share it with our readers. We extend our profound gratitude to

Richard M. Alderman, "The People's Lawyer", author of *Know Your Rights, Answers to Texans' Everyday Legal Questions*, Gulf Publishing;

Matrimonial attorney Cary B. Cheifetz of the law firm of Skoloff & Wolfe in Newark, NJ;

Matrimonial attorney Danielle de Benedictis, Boston, for the woman's perspective;

James Donnelly, Jr. for his expertise in closely-held businesses, and Andrew B. O'Donnell, for tax, estate and business planning, both of the law firm Mirick, O'Connell, DeMallie & Lougee in Worcester, MA;

Margorie Engel co-author of *The Divorce Decisions Workbook*, McGraw Hill, for her broad knowledge of marriage and divorce issues;

Michael Eschelbacher, Neil Rossman and Jeffrey Rossman of Rossman, Rossman and Eschelbacher, Boston, for their expertise in corporate and matrimonial law;

William Friedler, Esq., of Gordon and Friedler, Boston, for his expertise in estate planning and Q-Tip trusts;

Michelle Gianni, of the law firm, Suisman, Shapiro, Wool, Brennan and Gray, New London, CT;

Stephen C. Glassman, Esq. for his expertise in military and federal issues as related to matrimonial law, of Bonner & O'Connell, Washington, DC;

The Honorable Edward M. Ginsburg, probate court justice, Commonwealth of Massachusetts;

Peter F. Harrington, Esq., Newton, MA;

Attorney Pamela Hultin, of the law firm, Kaufman & Cumberland, Cleveland;

Acknowledgements (continued)

Attorney Alexander A. Bove, Jr., financial columnist, *The Boston Globe*

Monroe Inker, who literally "wrote The Book" on divorce law, of the law firm White, Inker, Aronson, Boston;

Brett K. Kates, Esq., author of *The Insider's Guide to Complete Asset Protection*, Dearborn/Enterprise Publishing;

Sanford Katz, Esq., Professor of Law, Boston College;

John Monticone, CPA, Medford, MA for his insights on tax issues;

Pension experts Franklin E. Peters, F.S.A. and Thomas P. Tierney, F.S.A., of Tierney & Peters, Natick, MA;

Hanson Reynolds, Esq. of Foley, Hoag and Eliot, Boston;

Stephen Small, author of *Preserving Family Lands* and Richard W. Mable for his knowledge of child support issues, both of the law firm, Powers and Hall, Boston;

John Ventura, bankruptcy attorney and author of *Fresh Start*, Dearborn Financial Publishing;

Attorneys Barbara Wand and Wayne Miller of the law firm, Hill and Barlow, in Boston for their expertise in pension matters;

Martin Whitney, of Benetech, Inc. in Wellesley, MA for his expertise in qualified retirement plans;

For their comprehensive knowledge of insurance issues, Joseph Pulitano and William Haggarty.

Special thanks to our dedicated support team: Liza Daniel, Jodi O'Rourke, Betsy Muller, John Nagy, and John Hannan; Cindy Burke and Sally Ford, two of the best paralegals in the business...also Vera Lee, Ramona and Jim Daniel for outstanding editorial support...And speaking of support, we owe a big debt of gratitude to Charlie Winton, Mark Oiumet and the rest of the Publishers Group West family.

... and utmost appreciation to our families and friends who endured the rigors of our literary pursuits with patience and encouragement, especially Carolyn, Lily, Ben and Emily; Steve and Jake.

We thank you all.

FOREWORD

Americans, who make more of marrying for love than any other people, also break up more of their marriages, but the figure reflects not so much the failure of love as the determination of people not to live without it.

–Morton Hunt

There is no surprise more magical than the surprise of being loved: It is God's finger on man's shoulder.

— Charles Morgan

THE NUMBER ONE REASON that people marry, whether for the first, second, or tenth time, is LOVE. Love is such an exalted treasure that one would have to be a heartless cynic to say anything bad about it. Shall we begin?

First, love is too perishable. It is routinely snuffed out by day-to-day clashes with life's inequities and adversities.

Second, love isn't enough. The fact that you are reading this book is ample evidence that you already know that truth. What assurance do you have that your next journey along the path of matrimony will lead you to a better destination than your last? Certainly not love.

And third, love is painful — sometimes during the entire reign of its thrall, but certainly its death is exquisite torture. When you stand alone with the shambles of a wrecked marriage around your ankles and face the agony of being "I" not "we", you swear that you will never risk such suffering again. So why on earth are you planning to get remarried?

Marriage is our last, best chance to grow up.

— Joseph Barth

LOVE ASIDE, THE OLD conventional wisdom held that women married to be taken care of financially in their old age, men to be taken care of physically and emotionally. Today women have careers too, and today men know all about nurturing their inner child. And we're enlightened now so that we think of modern marriage not as a barter of security and services but rather as a shared journey of the heart on the path of self-actualization and personal fulfillment.

Like many homilies, however, the old view reflected a timeless truth, as recent studies readily demonstrate: Married women do face fewer financial hardships than their single counterparts; and married men do experience longer, healthier, happier lives.

Companionship, regular sex in this age of AIDS, a need for the comforts of home and hearth, all add powerful incentives to take the leap again. But next time it will be different. We are not now who we were before.

When we married for the first time we believed in happily ever after, till death do us part. A future of endless tableaux stretched before us — scrubbed faces of little children eating pancakes 'round the breakfast table, our own faces beaming at graduations and weddings, our grandchildren playing on the swing set.

We saw ourselves smiling as we grew old and gray together and holding hands as we looked back over a fruitful lifetime. There would be troubles, we knew, but we blithely assumed that love conquers all. Ah, bitter reality: Half of all first marriages end in divorce.

The end of a marriage is a loss of innocence, a falling from grace, a betrayal of our trust that the universe is fair and sensible. For months or years after, we stagger through our daily lives clutching our psychological wounds, bleeding internally, bravely pretending to be "normal" when what we are is completely lost and alienated. "The divorced person is like a man with a black patch over one eye," said writer Jo Coudert. "He looks rather dashing but the fact is that he has been through a maiming experience."

Divorce is open-heart surgery performed with a meat cleaver. In recovery, we work at making sense of our ordeal and in time become reconciled. Bit by bit, our shroud of pain peels away and we emerge tender and tentative. We even begin to believe we could try again. Eventually we meet someone and, in a triumph of hope over experience, three-quarters of us remarry.

Ah, bitter pill: The failure rate for second marriages is as high as for first-timers. Understanding now that love does not conquer all, we are deeply disappointed in the accuracy of our revised perspective. Nevertheless, some of us try again. And even again. And so we have become a society of sequential monogamists.

That's why you need this book. It is designed to be something of an insurance policy. It deals at the outset with what most surveys identify as the roughest battleground in marriage: MONEY. We will look unflinchingly at every aspect of the subject so that when a problem arises, as it certainly will, both partners can say with composure, "We were prepared for something like that."

TABLE OF CONTENTS

CHAPTER 1

SPEAKING OF MONEY–WHY IT'S SO HARD

Many people feel that talking about money with their romantic partner is about as comfortable as going to the dentist for a root canal. That attitude alone is the cause of some of the thorniest problems in relationships.

IT IS A TIRESOME TRUISM BORNE OUT IN SURVEY after survey: Good communication makes for good marriages. In pursuit of intimacy, loving partners try hard to put that concept into practice. We've gotten good at discussing all kinds of formerly taboo subjects: our childhood traumas, our addictions, our shames. The era of sexually transmitted diseases has even taught us to be good at discussing sex.

Unfortunately for our romantic relationships we seem not to have made much progress with the last taboo: talking about money. Take the case of Laurie and Bob:

Laurie, a divorced mother, met Bob, a divorced father. They fell madly in love and married a year later. At the time Laurie knew how much money Bob earned but had no idea how much support he paid to his children and ex-wife. She never discussed with him whether she would contribute her salary to living expenses or save it for luxuries. Bob never asked her how she planned to pay for her son's college tuition, how much her pension was worth, whether her child support payments came on time.

What's surprising is that Bob is a successful businessman who's adept at financial negotiations and Laurie is a family lawyer who knows firsthand the problems money can cause in a marriage. So why didn't these two sophisticated adults talk about money before they got married?

Laurie is almost embarrassed by the explanation. "I re-married late; I was 48. It was such a big step, I was afraid of blow-

ing it. Maybe it's superstitious, but I thought talking about his income, his assets, my income, my assets, what happens if we don't stay married — it was like a jinx. It would make the worst come true." Bob's reason: "*I was afraid she'd think I was materialistic.*"

Bob and Laurie are not alone. We all know that we should talk about money with those nearest and dearest but most of us avoid the subject at all costs.

Eight Common Myths About Love and Money

ONE WOULD THINK that going through the financial, let alone emotional, trauma of a divorce would wipe out our inhibitions about money. Not necessarily. The subject is fraught with bugaboos that don't die easily. Here are some of the fearful myths we harbor that cause us to avoid the subject with the people we love most:

1. Talking about what will happen if we get a divorce is bad luck.

FALSE, OF COURSE. However, if you can't resolve whatever disagreements come up in your discussions, you may decide to postpone or even cancel your wedding plans. Wouldn't you rather know you have irreconcilable differences before you get married than go through a painful and costly divorce?

2. Talking about money destroys romance.

FALSE. TRUE CLOSENESS is based on being accepted for who we are. Your partner needs to know about you, and your attitude toward money is one facet. Are you a careful spender? Do you like to splurge occasionally? What money problems do you worry about? What do you hope to be able to accomplish and what financial resources will it take to get there? The more you trade information and resolve differences, the more trust you will build together.

3. Talking about money turns the relationship into a business partnership.

TRUE. MARRIAGE is a lot of things, including a business partnership. And there's nothing wrong with that as long as the other parts are given equal attention. A good business partnership is fun, challenging and rewarding — things that also make up a good marriage.

4. If we really love each other, all our money should go into the same pot.

FALSE. MANY LOVING couples keep their finances separate and find it is easier to manage that way. Whether or not you decide to combine all your assets and income has nothing to do with how much you love or trust each other. In many cases, from a practical standpoint combining finances can have dire consequences.

5. A prenuptial agreement can't take into account all the things that might happen in the future so there's no reason to bother with it.

FALSE. YOUR AGREEMENT is just a blueprint. Many couples agree to review their contract periodically (once a year, every three years or more) and make whatever changes new circumstances warrant. Some even go away on a weekend vacation just for that purpose. If you are already married and financial issues come up that you want to clarify you can even write up a post-marital agreement.

6. Where there's lots of money there are no problems.

FALSE. YOU MAY HAVE lots of money and spend even more. Both of you need to know not only how much is coming in but also how much is going out and where it's going.

7. Money problems work themselves out if you really love each other.

FALSE. THAT'S WHY money is always at the top of the list of problems leading to divorce. Money problems that don't get discussed and resolved have a way of destroying love.

8. Talking about my desires regarding money will make me appear selfish.

FALSE. ON THE CONTRARY, it's a sign of maturity to be comfortable expressing your needs and asking for what you want. When both partners do that, they have the basis for open, honest discussion. When people are afraid to talk, they could end up feeling deprived, resentful and mistreated simply because their partner didn't know what they wanted.

The New Pillow Talk: Finances

CONTRARY TO POPULAR myth money talk does not destroy intimacy. Actually, quite the reverse is true. Money is a very intimate subject. It is emotionally loaded, private, deeply personal. Money is tied to our feelings, our childhood experiences good and bad, our self esteem, our fears about how others see us, our hopes and expectations for the future. With all that baggage on the subject, it's no wonder we have trouble discussing it.

As with sex, however, current events are forcing us to learn how to overcome the "unmentionableness" of money in romantic situations.

How do you begin to talk about money? Read this book and then sit down and talk.

THE PURPOSE OF THIS book is to introduce you to ideas about marriage and money that you may never have considered before. We will look at a broad range of issues; some will be relevant to your situation, some not, or at least not right now. As you read, some topics may pose particular difficulties for you and your partner. We will try to suggest options to help you work through problems in the smoothest, fairest way possible.

The people who need this book, as the title suggests, are those who are planning to remarry. Generally these folks are older and have acquired both assets and responsibilities. But any couple with assets and responsibilities, whether marrying for the first time or already married for years, can benefit from the information contained here. However, the very best time to deal with the issue of money is before you get married. After all, it's always easier to separate an egg *before* you scramble it.

It's best that both partners read this book, and as you do keep a pencil in hand to make notations in the margins whenever you see something that relates to your own concerns. When you've both finished, agree on a time to sit down to discuss the areas you've each marked. If there are several thorny issues, discuss only one and set another time to handle the next topic. There may be disagreements. Don't expect to resolve them the first time around.

Each side must be willing to work hard to be fair and to respect the other's needs and insecurities. After all, in your new life together you may encounter unexpected problems as well as happiness. It's natural to feel scared. Both sides also must be clear about what they need to feel financially secure in the marriage. And both must be open to accepting new and unfamiliar solutions.

You are essentially embarking upon a negotiation process. The goal, when it's over, is to have a clear and comfortable understanding of how money will be handled in your marriage. This book is a tool to get the dialogue going.

We are not recommending that you do it yourself, however. You probably won't resolve all your issues just by reading this (or any other book). Many of the chapters deal with complicated issues that need sophisticated planning to be resolved effectively. But at least you will have identified the areas you want to work on.

The next step is to call for help. To take advantage of the information you acquire, you may well need a professional. In fact, you may need more than one professional — a financial planner, accountant, insurance broker, matrimonial lawyer, business lawyer, tax and estate planning specialist or pension expert. If you've found it hard to talk about some issues, a marriage counselor also could be in order.

If that seems like a lot of fees to pay, look at it this way: It's undoubtedly far less than you'd have to pay to clean up a mess if something were to go wrong. There is no cheaper time to use experts. Besides saving you money they can save you disappointment and much grief.

CHAPTER 2

PRENUPTIAL, POSTMARITAL AGREEMENTS — A TOUCHY SUBJECT

To get married is to tie a knot
with the tongue that you cannot
undo with your teeth.

—E.M. *Wright*

ALMOST EVERYBODY FEELS UNCOMFORTABLE about premarital agreements, even lawyers who routinely recommend them to clients. Although they know full well the hazards of matrimony, they are as likely as lay people NOT to use one themselves. The folks who are enthusiastic about them are the financial advisors to the rich and famous — most of their clients use them. Wealthy people stay that way because of their sharp advice. There's a lesson there for the rest of us.

The purpose of this chapter is not to convince you that you need a marital agreement. By the time you get to the end of this book, you will have convinced yourself of their benefits. For now, it's necessary for you at least to understand what they are because we're going to be referring to them in the following chapters.

Marital Contracts 101

MARRIAGE IS AN ECONOMIC partnership in which there are always trade-offs. Each partner brings certain elements in different proportions and all combine to form a relationship that is, one hopes, mutually beneficial. Here's what most men and women bring to the marital table:

- assets (property, investments, a business, advanced degrees, licenses)

- earning ability (skills, experience, career network)
- services (homemaking and childrearing, home maintence and remodeling)
- liabilities (debts, back taxes)
- responsibilities (children and support obligations from a previous marriage)
- future prospects (inheritances, pensions)

Striking a balance

A MARITAL CONTRACT SEEKS to create a framework for balancing the contributions of each partner and spells out what will happen in the event of death or a divorce. If they are written before the marriage, they are called prenuptial, premarital or antenuptial agreements. Agreements cover four basic issues:

- **Tagging assets and liabilities** What assets do you each bring? How much are they worth? Who owns them now? Which ones will become marital property and which will continue to be owned by either party individually? What about gifts and inheritances? Will they be shared or kept separate? What liabilities do you each bring, such as back taxes or other debts?
- **What happens if you get a divorce?** Will there be alimony? A lump sum payment? Will you split or

exempt appreciation of assets brought to the marriage? How will you divide assets purchased from joint funds?

- **Planning your estates** Who gets what after the death of either spouse? What will go to children from a previous marriage or children you may have in the future?
- **Evening the score** How will you compensate for special contributions such as one party limiting a career or losing pension benefits because of child-rearing responsibilities? Or conversely, how to compensate for one spouse bringing in more liabilities.

The purpose of marital agreements

IF YOU DO NOT HAVE A prenuptial agreement and you get a divorce the laws of the state will determine what you will be left with.

In the past 20 years, all states have adopted one of two models for dividing the marital pie. Nine states (Arizona, California, Idaho, Louisiana, Nevada, New Mexico, Texas, Washington and Wisconsin) go by community property law that holds that all assets and liabilities acquired during a marriage belong equally to both parties and are to be divided in half in the event of a divorce. The remaining states operate under the premise of equitable distribution, meaning fundamentally that what's yours is yours, what's mine is mine. But the court in those states has wide discretion in shifting things around to achieve "equity" or fairness. What's fair? Whatever the judge thinks is fair!

The rules are often inflexible; in many instances the system is basically one-size-fits-all, or rather one size fits nobody very well. Here are two examples of the laws at work:

Suppose you get married and a month later drop dead without a will. Under the law in some states, your spouse gets half of everything you own. What if you have six children from your last marriage including a severely disabled son who needs constant care? Tough luck. For one month of marriage, your widow gets half your assets and the six kids divide the rest.

Or let's say you live in a community property state. You've owned a home for many years. The mortgage is paid off and the property is now worth $200,000. Your new spouse moves in and you put her name on the deed. Within a year, the marriage falls apart. Under the law, your spouse gets half of your house. You can come up with $100,000 to buy her out or you can sell the home you cherish.

These situations show what happens when the rules don't bend. Yet, where judges are allowed to interpret (or bend) the rules, the outcome can be equally unfair. Take the case of the woman who married a man with two post graduate degrees who sat around the house all day drinking beer and playing his guitar while she worked overtime to support him and their two kids. When they divorced the judge gave him half of her pension.

The purpose of a premarital agreement is to design a better fitting set of rules by 1) preempting state laws and 2) preventing a judge from exercising too much discretion. By drawing one up, a couple can largely take control into their own hands and out of the state's.

If *you* want to decide what's fair — and not be subject to some blind set of laws — the means to that end is a marital contract. But you must be very careful in drafting it or it will not hold up in court. This is definitely not a do-it-yourself project. You need professional help to get it right.

A watertight agreement? PREMARITAL AGREEMENTS HOLD up in court only when they meet certain conditions. These are:

- **Full disclosure of all financial information** The quickest way to invalidate the contract is to to hide any of your assets. If the marriage doesn't work out and your spouse uncovers assets that you did not declare in your prenuptial agreement, the whole contract could be thrown out. Lawyers who draw up prenuptial agreements for wealthy clients are such sticklers on this point that they often advise clients to pad their net worth rather than minimize it.

Usually both parties exchange financial statements listing all assets and sources of income. You must also be thorough about disclosing any debts and financial obligations like alimony, child support or back taxes (see Worksheets, back of book).

- **Fair and reasonable terms** Unlike commercial contracts, the law requires that marital contracts meet the criteria of fairness. For instance, suppose you rent an apartment for $1000 a month and later find out that your neighbors who have identical apartments pay only $500. You may think your landlord is not being fair but since this is a commercial contract you probably would not have your rent lowered by suing.

  But in marital contracts if the court thinks that the deal a couple struck was significantly unfair to one party the whole thing can be thrown out. Taken all together, the contract must represent a reasonable arrangement given your individual assets, your ages, intelligence, earning capacity, and business sense. In addition, many states require that you also take into consideration the health of both parties, their prior standard of living and possibly their children, past and future.

- **No pressure** The court is likely to throw out any agreement that it determines was made under emotional stress, physical or mental disability, or threat of force. Many lawyers now videotape the signing of the contract to show that both sides were fully aware of what they were doing and acted of their own free will. Threatening not to marry someone unless she signs an agreement may be construed as duress, however. Coercion is in the eye of the beholder as this story demonstrates.

Fred, a wealthy building contractor, had a soft spot in his heart for beautiful redheads and it was giving him a soft spot in his wallet. His first two wives cleaned him out so when he fell the next time, he knew he wanted a prenuptial agreement.

Afraid his beloved would be angry when he told her, he waited until a week before the wedding to hand her the contract. He couldn't go through with the marriage without this, he told her, flushed with embarrassment. She was afraid that if she protested he would call off the wedding so she signed. Five years later, when the marriage fell apart, the wife's lawyer argued she signed under duress because Fred had threatened to cancel the wedding. The judge agreed and tossed out the agreement.

This story illustrates why it is important to talk about money well before the wedding date. Fred may not have meant to pull a fast one on his bride but his awkwardness did have the effect of pressuring her in a manner the court considered unfair. Had he given her plenty of time to think about the prenuptial agreement and to talk over her options with a lawyer, it probably would have held up.

WARNING Marital agreements can become stale. What was fair the day you got married could be completely lopsided a few years later. The birth of children that requires one spouse to leave work, for instance, or a move that is advantageous to one spouse and detrimental to the other are two instances of changes that could affect the fairness of the agreement. Once the balance shifts, a court is likely to void the contract and the judge's determination of fairness, not yours, will prevail. Premarital agreements should be routinely reviewed and updated every few years or after significant events like the birth of a child or a change in economic circumstances.

Even with all these criteria met, premarital agreements are no guarantee that things will go exactly as planned. One lawyer who has handled many divorces for clients who had them says she has never seen one come through the court process without alteration. Even so, she says, the outcome was much closer to what the parties originally intended than would have occurred without one.

How to do it wrong: Do it yourself

FAMOUS LAST WORDS: "We're in love. We don't have any problems. We can do it ourselves." The excitement of the moment can mask future difficulties. Prenuptial agreements drawn up without a lawyer's help may or may not hold up. While the courts have even recognized the validity of oral prenuptial contracts, judges have the authority to toss out an agreement that doesn't measure up to their standards. There are too many variables that a professional would know to look out for that you could miss.

For instance, under Texas law a divorce court cannot award alimony. Suppose a women is planning to give up a lucrative career to care for her future husband's three children. If the marriage doesn't work out she knows it may take years to get her career back on track. She feels that she would need alimony during that period. The best time to deal with the issue is before the marriage in a prenuptial contract. Although in Texas the court can't award alimony, it could be enforced once it's part of their prenuptial contract.

Another anomaly: In virtually every state an inheritance is considered the property of the person who receives it. Not so in Connecticut. If you don't specifically exempt it in a prenuptial agreement, it is at risk in a divorce.

Because of these and other tricky legalities, marital contracts must be drawn very carefully. A judge is more likely to recognize a contract drawn up by a professional than a homemade job full of holes.

There are a number of self-help premarital agreement kits on the market. They may be a great way to get a discussion going with your mate but they are not definitive or complete or even up-to-date. Don't stop there; see a professional. You need current information because the law is always changing and there may be issues important to you that are not covered in any generic source (even this book).

A big mistake: having one lawyer represent both parties

ATTORNEYS WHO REPRESENT wealthy clients absolutely insist that each side, especially the less wealthy affianced, have his or her own counsel. If the couple ever ends up in court, the spouse who signed without legal representation can claim that unfair advantage was taken by the lawyer who drew up the contract.

There's a real benefit to having two lawyers draw up your prenuptial agreement: The bride and groom don't have to haggle and possibly destroy the atmosphere of trust and optimism that should prevail at this happy time. One matrimonial lawyer, in fact, always avoids having the couple in the same room with their lawyers during the negotiation process because the issues that could come up are so sensitive. One of the most painful contingencies that must be covered is, What happens if we get a divorce?

Most couples, he says, have a hard time with that issue; it's actually easier for them to talk about, What happens if one of us dies? People accept death as inevitable, he maintains, but the prospect of another divorce is more threatening because it is associated with failure, not fate.

Pondering the imponderable: Divorce

HERE ARE TWO EXAMPLES of the sensitive points your lawyers may need to work out involving, What happens if you get a divorce?

- Will there be alimony or will it be waived in this agreement? If both partners are financially able to take care of themselves, both may agree that alimony is unnecessary. But if the wife, for instance, expects to stay home to care for young children she may insist that she would need financial help to get back on her feet. But will the help take the form of alimony or a lump sum payment? The lawyer for the husband may advise a cash settlement rather than alimony. The husband would pay more at the beginning but generally there's less risk for him because the book is closed once he's paid up. The wife's lawyer would probably advise alimony because she can go back to court later to ask for more money if her circumstances change for the worse.
- If you divorce, who will pay the legal fees? In one important way, a working husband has traditionally been in a much better position to handle a divorce than his stay-at-home wife. He has cash flow; she does not. A court may order him to pay interim support but chances are she won't have enough money to pay a lawyer. She may need to borrow from her family or agree to pay the fees later out of whatever settlement she gets. She certainly will be in no posi-

tion to hold out for a more favorable settlement. A better idea is to agree to seek divorce mediation to resolve differences. It's much less expensive, less adversarial, less damaging emotionally to both sides. The spouse who is earning an income can agree to pay all or a large portion of the cost, and the amount would likely be much less than a divorce lawyer. With this arrangement the spouse with less money would not be pressured into accepting an unfair settlement.

- If you divorce, who stays in the house? Before no-fault and equitable distribution laws, wives were awarded most of the marital property and custody of the children. Generally a wife could expect to keep the family home which enabled her and the children to sustain a stable home life after the marriage ended.

  Today, courts often order that the house be sold and the proceeds divided immediately. Often the wife can't buy another home because she doesn't have enough cash for a down payment or income to qualify for a mortgage. The social and psychological disruption of moving can be especially traumatic for children.

> An alternative is to agree in the prenuptial contract that if the marriage ends while the children are young, the wife will be allowed to stay in the home with the husband's name remaining on the deed. Better yet, put the house in a trust to protect it from creditors. Everybody benefits by this arrangement. The husband knows that his investment is protected. The children are secure in their own home. And the wife effectively has a lien on the home as protection against default on spousal or child support. (Obviously, if the husband is the custodial spouse, the situation could be reversed.)

This kind of creative problem avoidance can make for a kinder, gentler divorce, if such is possible. But you need to find good lawyers who understand what should be covered and how to handle their clients with sensitivity.

Pick lawyers who can build bridges rather than walls

WITH THE COUPLE OUT of the direct negotiations, their lawyers can work out sensitive issues without destroying their clients' romantic relationship. Throughout the process, the bride and groom can say to each other, "You know I'll love you forever, but my lawyer wants to have this clause in here. You know how lawyers are."

Obviously, you will both want to pick lawyers who understand that protecting their client should not require adversarial tactics. When choosing an attorney, talk over your concerns and try to get a sense of whether he/she has the requisite sensitivity and compassion. If you don't feel comfortable, keep looking. Many lawyers do not charge for the initial visit (ask when you schedule the interview). Get referrals from friends or see Resources, Lawyers. Shop around until you find someone who "feels" right to you.

Providing for children

YOU MAY NOTICE that there's been little mention of providing for children in a prenuptial agreement. In the event of a divorce, a court would undoubtedly review the needs of children wholly independently of whatever you had agreed to between yourselves. The court's primary consideration is, What's in the best interest of the children? You certainly may express your wishes in your agreement. The court will be less likely to overrule them if the children are being well-served.

The lifestyle issues

ALTHOUGH A MARITAL contract primarily covers financial

arrangements, some people feel sufficiently strongly about "lifestyle" issues that they want them written in too. These issues can be serious ones like: How many children will you have? In what religion will they be raised? How do you each feel about the possibility of an abortion? What part of the country will you live in?

Or, they can be more mundane but potentially maddening, such as: Who will do the housework? Who will pay for a cleaning service? For day care? How many family vacations will be spent with each set of in-laws? Some people even write in who gets custody of the dog if the marriage ends. If you know that certain issues have the potential to cause major problems or just drive you nuts in slow motion, there's nothing to stop you from resolving them in your prenuptial agreement.

POSTmarital agreements

A NEW KIND OF MARITAL agreement is gaining popularity, one that is drawn up after the wedding. Not just an updating of a prenuptial agreement, the postmarital contract is an original. At some time during the course of a marriage a couple may wish to spell out contractually the kinds of things that would have been covered in a prenuptial. A number of events could trigger the need to do this, for instance:

- One partner, let's say the husband, has a business that is doing well. He wants to be sure that his children take over the business when he dies or retires. He asks his wife to waive her interest in the business. If the couple gets a divorce, it is not part of the marital pie; if he dies, she does not inherit a portion of it.
- One partner, the wife, for example, wants to leave all her assets to her children when she dies. She asks her husband to waive his legal rights to her estate.
- One partner, the wife again, learns that she will inherit a large piece of property from her family. She wants to be sure her children from a previous marriage inherit it when she dies. If she gets a divorce, in some cases the property might be considered a marital asset and be split up. If she dies, a portion of the property could go to her spouse, not her children. So she asks her husband to agree that the property is not a marital asset and to waive his right to inherit any of it if she dies first.
- The couple is moving from a community property state (where, under the law, each spouse owns half the assets) to an equitable distribution state (where assets tend to be considered the property of who-

ever's name appears on them). Years ago, the husband had put the family home in his wife's name to protect it from possible lawsuits arising from his business. When they move he would be going from owning half a house to owning nothing. He wants to be sure that he protects his interest in the house.

- One spouse, the husband, for instance, has been fooling around. His wife, feeling very vulnerable now, insists that as a consideration for her taking him back he set aside a certain portion of his assets for her. An offbeat case of this sort occurred some years ago:

Justine was married to a big real estate developer known in his flashy advertisements as "Ken Korn, the Kondo King". When his wife caught him in the arms of another woman Ken was smitten with remorse. Desperate to win her back, in a postmarital agreement he signed over to her all his condo holdings. The new ads read "Justine Korn, the Kondo King".

The same rules apply to postmarital contracts as to prenuptial ones: full disclosure, fairness, lack of duress, representation for both parties. Postmarital contracts are relatively new for most courts so it is particularly important that you enlist the services of professionals with experience in matrimonial law.

Some courts still will not honor postmarital contracts, largely a holdover from the days when women didn't have the right to enter into contracts or own property in their own names and when all rights in a marriage belonged to the husband.

The purpose of a postmarital contract, like one written before the wedding, is to design a better-fitting set of rules than those provided by the state. These contracts have been around for only a few years so as yet there is little case law to back them. Therefore, it is especially important that you get the help of professionals familiar with your state's laws governing marriage and divorce.

A marital contract, whether drawn before the wedding or after, spells out the answer to the question, What am I getting myself into? It can't eliminate all risks but it can greatly minimize many of them. Moreover, it can give you the peace of mind that comes from good communication and careful planning with your partner.

CHAPTER 3

CREDIT: HIS & HERS, FOR RICHER, FOR POORER?

The financial pitfalls facing the remarried are numerous and varied. Fortunately, avoiding some of them can be quite simple, once you understand the potential problems. One of the most important things you can do is to keep your credit separate.

Why you should have separate credit

YOU CAN SHARE A BED, you can even share your toothbrush, but you should not share credit cards with your spouse. It's not a matter of trust. It's a precaution in case of hard times. You or your spouse may run into financial problems — an illness, a job layoff, a bad recession that affects one more than the other. When money gets tight, separate accounts allow you to work together as a couple to preserve your good credit. Here's an example:

Separate credit protects you from each other's creditors.

LET'S SAY MARK loses his $40,000 a year job and is unable to find an equivalent one. Janet's salary isn't enough to keep up with their expenses. Naturally, they want to protect as much of their good credit as possible. His income has historically been more than hers, a situation they expect will return when he gets a new job. For this reason, they decide it's more important to preserve his credit than hers.

So while Mark is mailing resumes and going to interviews, they agree to use Janet's salary to pay his charge card bills on time and to cover their two most critical bills, their mortgage and health insurance. Then knowing that medical bills generally do not show up on a credit report they notify the doctor and dentist that they will be unable to pay those bills on time. They sell their boat and Mark's motorcycle.

At this point Janet's payments on her car loan and credit cards are falling far behind. By the time Mark gets another job, her good credit history is history. As for Mark since he was not a signer on her obligations, his credit is intact. He finally does get a new job. With his greater earning power, he is able to continue to carry his obligations and also take out a small debt consolidation loan to pay off Janet's back bills. She will be able to rehabilitate her credit over time but meanwhile they will get along on Mark's.

WARNING If you run into hard times, it is important to have separate credit. It's also a good idea to keep assets, checking and savings accounts separate since those in one partner's name alone cannot be garnished by the other's creditors.

By the way, this is a good instance of a postmarital agreement (see Chapter 2) making sense. Janet is assuming all the risk in this situation. In fairness to her, they could write down what Janet is contributing to solving their joint problem and how Mark will compensate her when he is able. It needn't be a big deal, just a brief explanation signed by both of them. They may have complete confidence in each other and the durability of their marriage but gestures of clarity and fairness like this can only strengthen a relationship.

Separate credit protects you from each other.

WHEN A MARRIAGE doesn't work out, separate credit can also protect the spouses from each other. How? Because under the law either signer on a debt can be held responsible for 100 percent (not just half) of the total owed. That means if one doesn't pay his or her share, the other gets stuck for the whole amount. Given the animosity and irrationality that go with most divorces, joint credit is a potential disaster. A case in point — How not to do it:

When Elizabeth and Tony parted company after eight years of marriage, Elizabeth learned that her husband had run up over $40,000 in charges on their joint credit cards. She immediately notified the card companies that she would not be responsible for any further bills. Unfortunately, that did not help with the charges already there. Since they live in a community property state (Texas), in their divorce all assets and debts were divided down the middle. Although almost none of the charges were Elizabeth's, the court gave her responsibility for $20,000 of the debt.

Worse yet, her husband did not even pay his share and she began receiving dunning phone calls. The card companies explained to her that divorce settlements are not binding on creditors. Because her name was on the credit cards with her husband's, she was responsible for the entire amount when he defaulted.

If your credit cards are in your name only and your spouse's are the same, you will eliminate or greatly minimize the risk of ever being stuck with each others debts.

Debts acquired during marriage

STATES VARY IN THE ways they regard liabilities incurred by married people. In **community property states** (Arizona, California, Idaho, Louisiana, Nevada, New Mexico, Texas, Washington, and Wisconsin) both spouses are considered equal owners of property AND equally responsible for debts acquired *during* the marriage, no matter whose name is on what or who signed for it. If you want to have more control in these matters, a prenuptial agreement can "partition" assets and liabilities so that his remain his and hers remain hers. By isolating the risk, you reduce the possibility that a creditor will go after both spouses for the debts of one spouse. It also will protect you from each other's debts if the marriage ends.

In **equitable distribution states** (all states other than those named above) property and debts are generally regarded as belonging solely to the person who acquired them. However, divorce courts apportion assets and liabilities according to "fairness" not "equality". Lacking a prenuptial or postmarital agreement the court has wide latitude in deciding whose assets will be used to satisfy which debts. Wouldn't you rather settle these issues yourselves before problems arise?

Will my new spouse's bad credit history affect me?

MANY PEOPLE GO into remarriage with bad credit marks from their last marriage. During a divorce, one of the first casualties is the couple's finances. One or the other spouse may empty out a bank account or stop paying certain bills. The strain of additional expenses such as legal fees and separate living quarters can knock the budget for a loop. Credit card bills, car loan and mortgage payments fall behind. When the dust settles, one or both spouses may have bad blotches on their credit record which will stay there for up to seven years. Let's continue the previous example:

When Elizabeth remarried, she and her new spouse, Steve, planned to buy a house. Steve had enough money for the down-payment, but both he and Elizabeth would have to sign on the loan because they needed her income to carry the mortgage. Unfortunately, Elizabeth's credit was a mess. Steve had to help her financially until she was able to clean up the marks on her record. It was three years before they felt confident enough to apply for a mortgage.

WARNING Credit problems that either partner brings from the past can affect the credit worthiness of the next marriage.

Can my new spouse's previous divorce affect me financially?

YOU COULD GET STUCK WITH debts left over from your spouse's previous divorce. Although a second spouse is never obliged to pay such debts, effectively they hit both partners in their joint wallet.

Vera and Fred got a divorce. At the time they had $100,000 in assets and $50,000 in liabilities. In dividing up the marital pie, Fred asked to keep their house which had $75,000 in equity. To even things out he also agreed to assume $50,000 of their debts. Vera got $25,000 in cash, CDs and bonds. They each netted $25,000.

Vera remarried. She and second husband Gene bought a house using her $25,000 plus another $25,000 from Gene. They were house-poor but happy. Vera believed Fred could well afford to pay the debt he had assumed, yet he defaulted and the creditors went *after Vera. Result: she and Gene had to scramble to hang on to their new home. Although the debt fell only to Vera, and Gene had no responsibility to pay, their creditors couldn't care less about the source of their financial difficulties. Vera and Gene would have been wise to keep all assets out of her name until Fred finished paying off his obligations.*

WARNING Before you remarry it's imperative to have your lawyer check all divorce agreements, his, hers, as many as there are, for as far back as they go. Even if you can't correct a potential problem, it's better to know where your exposure lies so you can plan accordingly.

Business loans

WIVES AND HUSBANDS should be especially cautious about signing on each other's business loans. Here's why:

Mollie owned two successful beauty salons; her husband Arthur was a real estate developer. They lived the life of luxury until the day the bottom fell out of the real estate market. Mollie had developed her business out of cash flow and had never needed a bank loan. But Arthur was in hock up to his eyebrows and Mollie had co-signed on $1 million of his loans. When Arthur's company went under, so *did the marriage. Arthur couldn't pay so Mollie ended up responsible for the whole million. Even though her businesses were still doing well, there was no way she could ever pay off the debt. She had to declare bankruptcy.*

If one spouse is a risk taker (an entrepreneur, for instance, or even a big spender), the safest and fairest thing to do is to protect the more conservative spouse by keeping everything separate — especially new debt.

WARNING When you co-sign on a business obligation you sign on to the full liability, not just "your half".

When you keep your debts separate, if things go wrong both spouses need not suffer equally. Had Mollie been shielded from the onslaught of Arthur's financial problems, their marriage might not have been a casualty. Protecting her could have been quite easy because federal law allows one spouse to declare bankruptcy without including the other. The process only involves the assets and debts of the person seeking bankruptcy protection. By filing bankruptcy, Arthur could have gotten a fresh start without dragging Mollie down with him. This solution is usually possible only when separate finances are structured and carefully maintained from the beginning. Once your assets and liabilities are co-mingled, you'd have a hard task proving that your joint assets should not go to satisfy your spouse's debts.

Will my ex's bankruptcy affect me?

HERE'S AN EXAMPLE of how a poorly constructed divorce agreement can wreak havoc years later:

As part of their divorce settlement Sean gave Beth a promissory note for $10,000, her half of the equity in their vacation condo. But within three years Sean's irregular mortgage payments and a drop in real estate values had completely eroded the equity. When Sean declared bankruptcy, his obligation to Beth was cancelled. She would probably never see a penny of her $10,000.

20-20 hindsight: Here's how Beth's divorce agreement should have been structured: Federal bankruptcy laws allow debts between ex-spouses to be wiped out. Alimony, however, is not cancelled by bankruptcy. Had she taken $10,000 in alimony instead of (but not worded as "in exchange for") her half of the house, Sean would not have been able to discharge the debt. Or, alternatively Beth could have asked for additional, or different, safer collateral.

Bankruptcy procedure is governed by both federal and state laws. Federal laws are consistent all over the country; state laws vary widely. In some states bankruptcy is a relatively painless procedure. Take Texas: When filing, an individual can keep some very big assets — a home, IRA or pension, $30,000 in cash, and there is no wage garnishment (except for spousal or child support). Gloomy economic conditions there have forced into bankruptcy many responsible, even financially conservative people. In fact, in Texas the list of bankruptcy filers reads like a register of the state's biggest movers and shakers (including a former governor). This is true in other parts of the country as well, which explains why bankruptcy has lost much of its stigma.

WARNING Be aware that your ex's bankruptcy could wipe out what you were promised in your divorce settlement.

What if my ex owes back taxes for a year in which we filed jointly — Will the IRS come after me?

BANKRUPTCY DOES NOT discharge taxes due during the previous three years for which the debtor did not file a return or during the previous six years if fraud or evasion was involved. That means that your ex cannot just file bankruptcy and be absolved of liability. As a practical matter, however, the IRS goes wherever the money is. If *you* are where the money is, you are on the hook. Often, when bankruptcy is involved, the IRS will work out a settlement at the time assets are liquidated. You might have to work with your ex to be sure this happens.

Given the 100 percent increase in bankruptcy filings over the last 15 years, you should bear this possibility in mind when drafting marital agreements. Court-ordered alimony and child support as well as tax liabilities cannot be discharged by bankruptcy, but most other debts between spouses are not so protected. Whatever you agree upon in a prenuptial or postmarital agreement will probably stand up if properly drafted.

Repairing credit problems

THE AFTERMATH OF MANY divorces is a long period of rebuilding good credit that was destroyed when the marriage fell apart. When you remarry it's important to clean up any mess as soon as possible so you and your new spouse can get on with your lives.

If one spouse carries financial baggage in the form of a poor credit history or even a bankruptcy, it will affect both of you. Bad marks stay on your credit record for seven years; bankruptcy for up to ten. Credit difficulties, however, need not cause permanent problems. You can work as a couple to repair the damage. Here's how to do it:

- If you are having trouble meeting your bills, begin by talking with a representative of a reputable consumer credit counseling service. A good place to start: the National Foundation for Consumer Credit, Inc. (see Resources, Credit for more information.)

- Find a friendly bank and enlist the banker's support in rebuilding your credit. Smaller local banks or credit unions are your best bet; they tend to be community oriented. Open a savings account there and deposit money into it bit by bit until you have built up a nest egg of $500 or more. The bank can then lend you money with your savings frozen as security on the loan.

  Why should you borrow money when you already have it in the bank? To establish a record of borrowing and repaying in a timely fashion. That's the first step in reestablishing your credit-worthiness.

  You can use this same "secured debt" method to establish a good history on a credit card. There are companies that specialize in just this kind of arrangement (see Resources, Credit for more information).

- While you are establishing a new record, work on clearing up old glitches. Your credit history may be on file at several different credit bureaus — large, national companies and small, local ones. There may be files on each of you individually and on you both as a couple.

If you recently have been turned down for credit, the company reporting your credit history must provide you with a copy of your record at no charge. Just write and ask for it. If you have not been turned down you may have to pay a small charge. Begin by checking your file at one or more of the bigger companies: TransUnion, Equifax, etc. (see Resources, Credit).

Don't be surprised to find outright errors on your record. These are so common that Congress is currently working on legislation to make credit reporting agencies adhere to higher standards of accuracy. After all, people like you are not their customers, giant retailers are. They are notoriously slow and uncooperative in working with individuals.

Whether accurate or not, eliminating blemishes on your record can take months or years. If you find you are unable to get a piece of inaccurate information removed within a reasonable time, you may have to take drastic steps. One credit counselor suggests going to small claims court to sue the local branch of the credit bureau for damages. You may not collect any money but you'll probably get their attention and a correction of your problem.

Work with your creditors. If your debt at a local department store was charged off because of non-payment, call the store and speak with the credit manager. Explain that you are trying to clean up your record and make arrangements to pay off all or part of the balance over time in exchange for removing the mark from your file. Write a letter confirming this agreement.

If you can't get a bad mark removed, write a letter of up to 100 words explaining your side of the story. By law, the credit bureau must add it to your file. In community property states, both spouses are jointly and separately responsible for debts incurred by either. If your bad rating was due to your ex-spouse's negligence, be sure to put that in the record.

WARNING The purpose in going through all this hassle is to establish good credit for both of you individually. Get rid of all joint accounts and don't complicate your life by opening any new ones.

Here's a final example of how careful you must be to keep your credit records separate:

Ed died leaving $35,000 of unpaid charge card bills.

Although the cards were in his name alone, the credit card companies began dunning his widow, Jennifer, claiming that since the couple resided in a community property state, she was equally responsible. Jennifer refused to pay. Some months later when she tried to open a charge account at a local department store, she was turned down. When she examined her credit report, she found that her late husband's debts had been recorded under her name. At this writing, her lawyer is suing the card companies for libel on the grounds that they are knowingly spreading damaging, false information about her.

If you live in a community property state, be extra cautious to make sure that your credit history and that of your spouse are kept separate. Some experts advise that you check your credit record every six to twelve months no matter where you live to catch and correct errors before they do you harm.

Good credit is a necessity for acquiring life's essentials such as transportation (car loans) and housing (leases and mortgages). Guard it as you would any other valuable asset.

CHAPTER 4

PROTECTING YOUR ASSETS FROM GHOSTS OF THE PAST & BAD SURPRISES

If you've already been through one divorce, you probably took a heavy hit in the wallet. You are planning to try again but now you place a high value on risk assessment and management.

Remarriage is fertile ground for money conflicts.

IN REMARRIAGE, AS IN LIFE, there are no absolute guarantees. The most you can do is to minimize the risks by making sure that you retain as much control of your finances as possible. Then as long as you act with full awareness of the limits and consequences of your choices you are holding the reins. Should you at some point decide to sign over everything but your toothbrush to your new spouse, you certainly may. But what you have learned from your divorce is that if this marriage goes wrong the last people you want to control what's left of your assets are a judge and a couple of lawyers. Let's look at various ways you can protect your assets.

What assets are we talking about?

ASSETS, FOR THE PURPOSE of this discussion, are defined as things of value that have a person's name on them. These usually include:

- checking accounts
- savings accounts
- certificates of deposit
- stocks
- bonds
- treasury notes & treasury bills
- savings bonds
- vacation homes
- investment real estate
- automobiles
- boats
- campers

- recreational vehicles
- The biggest asset for most couples is their home. This is covered separately in Chapter 5.

Everything on this list could be put at risk when you remarry. Let's look at the three biggest threats to your assets:

Threat Number One: Another divorce

IF THE MARRIAGE RUNS into problems, you could both be a threat to each other. The last time around you learned too late that all your assets were up for grabs. Without planning, that risk will always be present.

How to minimize Threat Number One

WHAT HAPPENS TO YOUR assets if you get a divorce? Even though your assets are in your name alone they probably will be considered marital property and be subject to the judge's discretion for distribution. Even in equitable distribution states where, theoretically, mine is mine and yours is yours, the court may shuffle assets belonging to either partner when dividing up the marital pie.

The single most effective protection for both spouses should the marriage not work out is a prenuptial agreement. The contract may cover all of the assets listed above plus others that do not have a name on them, such as works of art, fine Persian rugs and jewelry. If you both have listed all your assets, fully disclosed their value, used no pressure tactics on each other, been fair to each spouse and up-dated your agreement from time to time as circumstances changed, a court will probably uphold the contract.

People become mean and irrational during a divorce, a fact you may already know too well. Drawing up a premarital agreement at a time when you are thinking clearly is the best protection you can have. In fact, it may even start the marriage off on solid ground and establish a healthy and effective framework for dealing with money matters in the future. (For more on prenuptial and postmarital agreements, see Chapter 2.)

Threat Number Two: A previous marriage

OBLIGATIONS FROM AN EARLIER marriage have a nasty way of turning up in a later one. This comes as a shock to most women who marry men with support obligations to their previous family. (An apology to those who may suspect sexism in the following discussion. For the sake of simplicity we've looked at the most common situation: where the man is responsible for alimony and/or child support. Of course, the genders could be reversed.)

Financial liabilities never get permanently corralled because an ex always has the option of going back to court to seek a better arrangement. Your assets can be sucked into your spouse's problems.

Even if your husband's ex seems reasonable and he has a workable financial relationship with her, you must think and act defensively. Things may be okay for now, but here are two words to chill your spine: college tuition. That is not to say that you may not choose to help provide for your stepchild's education. Once again, the question is, Who decides what's fair, you or a judge?

Your husband's support obligation is not permanently carved in stone. His ex can always ask for more by claiming that her financial circumstances have deteriorated while his have been enhanced by *your* financial resources! (For more on this, see Chapter 8.) If payments fall into arrears, the court could order that your jointly-held assets be liquidated to satisfy your husband's past obligations.

Many people only get divorced on paper. Both parties may drag along all kinds of emotional baggage. Wrangling over alimony and/or child support is an expression of unfinished business that can contaminate a subsequent marriage.

Threat Number Three: Old debts

OBVIOUSLY THE TWO OF YOU will be assuming new obligations. (For how to deal with them see Chapter 3 regarding keeping your liabilities separate.) But you may not realize that you could also be inheriting your new spouse's old debts, tax liabilities, business problems and lawsuits.

Money matters become much more complicated the second (or third, or whatever) time around. Whatever the source of the threats, there are ways to deal with all of them. Each requires a specific tactic.

We've seen that a premarital agreement is the best way to minimize Threat Number One (another divorce). As for the other two, support obligations to an ex and your spouse's old debts are basically the same; they are both creditors. Let's look at things you can do to protect yourself from ghosts of the past and bad surprises.

How to minimize threats from a previous marriage and old debts

THE EASIEST WAY TO HEAD off danger from either of these is to take a hard look at how you are going to "hold" your assets.

Most people don't realize that there are several ways to designate ownership of assets and that each offers specific advantages and disadvantages. Knowing the form of ownership that best suits your situation can mean the difference between preserving or losing your assets if things turn bad in the future.

The most common ways to hold assets are:

- **individually,**
- as **joint tenants,**
- **as tenants in common,** and
- **in trust for someone else.**

Let's look at each one and consider the advantages and disadvantages each affords.

Individually:
"John Smith"

SIMPLY PUT, YOUR NAME ALONE is on the account, title or deed.

Advantages

- Your spouse's ex can never attach your assets for back alimony, child support, or other debts or obligations from their marriage.

- Your spouse's old creditors (or new for that matter) cannot get your assets as long as you did not co-sign on the notes.
- Assets in your own name make it easier to establish and maintain your own credit.

Disadvantages

- Your own creditors have an easy shot at your assets.
- Your assets must go through probate when you die. If you don't have a will, the court, not you, will decide who gets them. Even with a will, any "aggrieved" relative, including your spouse, can take a crack at breaking it. In addition, since probate is a public procedure, the whole world will know your business.
- If you become incapacitated, and you have not made out a power of attorney (see Chapter 12), your spouse will need to go to court to get permission to manage your funds. This is time-consuming, expensive and intrusive on your privacy.

Joint Tenants: "John AND Mary Smith"

IN THIS TYPE OF OWNERSHIP, both spouse's names are on the ownership document. Typically transactions can be made only with both signatures. Upon the death of one spouse the assets pass immediately and automatically to the survivor.

Advantages

- Your spouse has no access to the assets without your permission.
- When you die, they go directly to your spouse and avoid probate.

Disadvantages

- Your own creditors have an easy shot at your share of the assets.
- If your spouse's ex is looking for more money, your share of the assets are included when determining what resources are available. At least half the assets could be taken by a probate or family court to pay delinquent alimony or child support. The ex's lawyer would undoubtedly argue that these assets actually belong entirely to your spouse and that your name is on them only for convenience! Result? All could be lost.

- If your spouse's old creditors try to get your assets the argument will also be that your name is on the account for convenience only. At least half the assets could be available to your spouse's creditors. Let's say a husband and wife hold investment real estate jointly. He owes federal or state taxes from before their marriage; she owes nothing. The government can simply file a notice of lien against their property at the local registry and the wife's share will be as tied up as her husband's.
- If you become incapacitated, your spouse cannot get the funds except with a power of attorney or by going to court to request a conservatorship.
- When one spouse dies, jointly held accounts or properties may not always go to the survivor. Let's say the wife dies and the assets typically would go to her husband. Her children could go to court and argue that Mom never intended for their stepfather to get them but rather that his name was on them only for convenience.

Tenants in Common: "John OR Mary Smith"

BOTH SPOUSE'S NAMES GO on the assets, as with joint tenancy. Unlike joint tenancy, however, typically only one signature is required for sale, transfer or withdrawal of assets and they descend to the heirs of the deceased, not to the surviving spouse.

Advantages

- Either partner has access to the assets at any time. Depending on circumstances, this could also be a disadvantage.
- If you become incapacitated, your spouse can get to the funds immediately without going to court to get a conservatorship. Therefore, no one knows your business or has a chance to contest the manner in which the funds are being used.

Disadvantages

- Your creditors have an easy shot at your assets.
- As with joint tenancy, if your spouse's ex is looking for more money your assets could be taken by a probate or family court to pay delinquent alimony and child support.
- As with joint tenancy, if your spouse's creditors try to get them at least half are at risk.
- If one of you dies without a will, a tenancy in common guarantees that one-half of the assets will go

> through the deceased's estate, with the accompanying delay and expense of probate. The law might pass assets to people neither of you would chose — such as estranged children.

Note: Many financial institutions treat certain assets such as savings accounts, checking accounts and CDs, as both tenants in common and joint tenancy accounts. Typically when you see the word "or" on an account, it means that when one owner dies, the survivor gets everything.

Other assets such as stocks, bonds and real estate are treated differently. When the word "or" is used with these types of assets it almost always designates tenants in common, which means that one-half goes through the estate and therefore is subject to probate. If the word "and" is used it means two signatures are required.

Yes, the foregoing is confusing. That's why you should seek an expert's advice when deciding how to hold valuable assets.

Holding assets with your children: "John Smith AND Margaret Smith" (daughter) or "John Smith OR Margaret Smith" (daughter)

THE OPTION OF HOLDING assets with grown children may be appealing to some people. The assets can be held either as joint tenants (AND) or as tenants in common (OR).

Advantages

- Your spouse's ex can never reach the assets.
- Your spouse's old creditors can never get the assets.
- Assets held as joint tenants with your children go directly to them when you die thereby avoiding probate and possible challenges by your spouse or your stepchildren.

Disadvantages

- Holding assets with your children is no guarantee that your spouse will not be able to claim an interest if you get divorced. The opposing lawyer's first argument will be that your child's name is on the assets for convenience (probably true).
- Whether held as tenants in common or joint tenants, the assets are easily available to your creditors.

- If the assets are held as tenants in common with your offspring rather than your spouse, upon your death half would go through your will, subjecting your heirs to the delays and expense of probate. If you have no will, assets would be divided under the laws of your state, possibly going where you wouldn't want them to go.
- If your child gets sued, a creditor could try to attach his/her interest in your assets. The attempt would probably fail, but who needs the problems?
- If your offspring gets divorced, you can bet that his/her soon-to-be ex would claim that your assets are part of their marital property and ask for half.

"In trust for" accounts: "Mary in trust for Edward" (son)

THIS TYPE OF OWNERSHIP is almost always used by people holding money for their children or grandchildren. In this example, Mary is the trustee and owner of the funds and Edward (her son) is the beneficiary who can get them only upon Mary's death.

Advantages

- The court can never attach your assets for your spouse's back alimony, child support, or other debts from a previous marriage.
- Your spouse's old creditors cannot get your assets as long as you did not co-sign on the notes.

Disadvantage

- If you get a divorce, assets owned by you are considered marital property and therefore subject to division (or at least a nasty fight).

"In trust for" accounts: "Mary in trust for John" (husband)

HUSBANDS AND WIVES rarely hold assets this way. There are circumstances, however, when it might be a good idea. For instance, Mary wants John to have all the assets immediately upon her death but John has creditors from a business that failed. If she holds the assets with her husband as joint tenants, his creditors could go after them. On the other hand, if she sets up the account "Mary in trust for John," there's no question who owns them — Mary does. John's creditors including his ex and the IRS have absolutely no claim on them. If a creditor were to go after John, she could simply take his name off the title.

Advantages

- Mary has the right at any time to remove John's name or do what she wants with the assets without his permission.
- When she dies the assets go to John and it is almost impossible for Mary's other heirs, such as children from a previous marriage, to argue that she really meant to leave the assets to them. Unlike a joint tenancy where Mary's children could argue that John's name was on the assets for convenience, holding them in trust for John is conclusive evidence that she intended him to inherit them.

Disadvantage

- If Mary gets into a legal battle, her creditors could go after all the assets, not just half, as would be the case if the assets were held with her spouse (either jointly or as tenants in common).

Q. So how should you hold your assets?

A. It depends on your goals.

- If you want to ***make sure that your assets go to your children when you die,*** hold them in trust for them.
- If you want to ***make sure that your assets go to your spouse when you die,*** hold them in trust for your spouse.
- If you want to ***make sure that the co-holder can get access to assets if you become ill,*** hold them as tenants in common.
- If you want to ***make sure that no one can get your assets without your permission,*** hold them in joint tenancy with two signatures required, or in trust for the person you ultimately want to inherit them.
- If you want to ***make sure your spouse doesn't get your assets in case of a divorce,*** get a premarital agreement because anything that has your name on it can be considered a marital asset.
- If you want to ***make sure your spouse's ex doesn't get your assets,*** hold them individually or in trust for your spouse or your ultimate heirs.

- If you want to ***make sure your spouse's creditors don't get your assets,*** hold them individually or in trust for your spouse or your ultimate heirs.

The expanded definition of the word "assets"

BEFORE WE LEAVE THE SUBJECT of assets, there's one more issue you should know about. In recent years the courts have begun to view assets in a much broader context. When during the marriage one partner earns a master's degree, Ph.D., medical license, license to practice law, possibly even a real estate license, it's value in increased earnings is considered a marital asset. In two recent divorce cases, one involving an actress, the other a comedian, courts have even ruled that stardom or "celebrity good will" is a marital asset in which the spouse is entitled to share. In another recent case involving a TV personality, a husband was awarded alimony based on the view that he had contributed to his wife's success, just as a wife would have done for a husband. While feminists may mourn that equality comes faster for men than women, this is a step toward evening the score in not uncommon situations such as the following:

Carmen put Julio through medical school by working two jobs. Three weeks after receiving his license to practice medicine, Julio moved out and filed for a divorce. The judge awarded Carmen $200,000 to be paid over ten years saying that Carmen was entitled to share in the enhanced earning capacity that she had helped to create.

That certainly seems fair. But what about this case? *Karen and Gil married right after high school. They agreed to put each other through college. After Karen graduated and began working, she encouraged Gil to go back to school. Gil declined the offer, saying he just wasn't the ambitious type. Karen decided to continue at her job and to pursue her education at night school. She eventually earned a Ph.D. When the marriage broke up, Gil's lawyer asked for a substantial cash settlement based on Karen's superior earning capacity.* Most people would see this as an unfair demand, yet it is not uncommon.

WARNING There are many times when one spouse is entitled to share in the benefits of the other's increased earning potential. But if you are concerned that some day you may unfairly have to part with a portion of the fruits of your own labors, get out of medical school, or whatever, before you get married.

CHAPTER 5

THE ROOF OVER YOUR HEAD — AND HOW TO KEEP IT THERE

The single most important asset you own is probably your house. It represents a substantial investment, the security of having a roof over your head, and the comforts of home and hearth. Either you or your partner may own a house that you will share after your wedding. Or you may be planning to buy one. If you have a romantic impulse to place both names on the deed to the home you live in together, think twice. You could be creating serious problems.

Whose name goes on the deed?

A FAMOUS MASSACHUSETTS case chillingly illustrates why you must use caution when deciding whose name goes on the deed to a home.

Roberta and Bill were divorced in 1970. Their separation agreement required that Bill pay Roberta $75 per week alimony. He kept up the payments for five years during which time he married Shirley. In year six his payments to Roberta fell into arrears.

Roberta filed a contempt petition claiming that Bill had failed to meet his obligation. In court Bill argued that he was unable to comply with the support agreement because his income had dropped dramatically.

The court didn't disagree that his income was down. However, it did look at what resources might be used to satisfy the obligation. Here's what it found: Bill and his second wife jointly owned a new house. Evidence showed that most of the money used to purchase and improve the home came from Shirley but Bill had contributed labor for remodeling. Although Bill was unemployed, Shirley was currently working.

The court ruled that although Bill's new wife had no obligation to contribute to his alimony payments, assets which she brought to the marriage or which they acquired together could and should be used to pay the alimony. Their house was just such an asset. Therefore, the court held that Bill was in contempt and could be jailed for failure to pay. Shirley was faced with selling or refinancing the house she paid for or see her husband go to jail.

WARNING A new wife has no legal responsibility to contribute to her husband's alimony or child support payments. However, if she puts her husband's name on the title to her home (or any other asset), she runs the risk that his ex could take it.

In the previous chapter we discussed various threats to your assets and how to deal with them. Although the threats to your home are essentially the same as those involving any other asset, there are special considerations involved in protecting it. Let's examine them.

The three biggest threats to your house:

- Number One: Another divorce
- Number Two: Your previous marriage (see example above)
- Number Three: Debts old and new

How to Minimize Threat Number One (Another Divorce)

IF YOU OWN A HOME that you are bringing into the marriage, the most important thing you can do is to make sure that your house remains your house in the event of a divorce. To guarantee this, draw up a prenuptial agreement stating that the house is your separate property. You also want to make sure that your property doesn't get inadvertently "transmuted" into community property. This can happen when both partners pay bills connected with the home with their separate and joint money. After a while, the question becomes, Whose property is this now?

To avoid confusion and risk in the event of a divorce, spell out in your prenuptial agreement how mortgage payments will be handled. For instance, if your spouse pays part of the mortgage, a judge could interpret that as equity in the house rather than rent. It might be better if the owner of the house paid the mortgage, out of his or her separate bank account. The other spouse can balance the situation by paying other household bills.

In most states you and your spouse share in any appreciation in the value of the house that occurs during the term of the marriage. In your prenuptial agreement you could choose to split the appreciation or exempt it altogether. In fairness you also should spell out that any monies your spouse pays into the house for remodeling or repairs will be reimbursed plus interest if the marriage ends.

How to protect your house from Threats Two and Three, an ex-spouse and other creditors

IN THE PREVIOUS CHAPTER we discussed various ways to hold assets in order to protect them. There are also a number of ways to hold this very special asset, your house. As with the others, each form of ownership has advantages and disadvantages.

There are three common ways the title of a house can be held: ***tenants in common, tenants by the entirety, or joint tenants.***

Tenants in common

IF THE TITLE READS "John and/or Mary Smith", with no other qualifying words (such as "jointly" or "as joint tenants"), then the ownership is a tenancy in common. Property held this way can be sold or transferred without the consent or knowledge of the co-holder.

Advantage

- In certain estate plans, this form ensures that there will not be a double tax on one-half the property.

Disadvantages

- Both owners have limited protection and control. Your partner can sell half interest in the house or give it away without your permission and you can do the same.
- Both owners' creditors (including an ex-spouse) can put a lien on the property, petition the court to cut up the property or force a sale of the entire parcel to get the proceeds of the debtor's share.
- You or your co-holder could petition the court to do all of the above too.
- When you die, your half goes through your estate to your heirs, not to the survivor on the deed, with the accompanying delay and expense of probate. Your widow(er) ends up owning the property with whomever you willed it to, a situation that could be difficult for all.

Joint tenants

THIS TITLE READS: "JOHN and Mary Smith, jointly" or "as joint tenants" or "as joint tenants with right of survivorship". Unlike tenants in common, in this form of ownership the coholders have an "undivided" interest in the property. That means when one owner dies his share goes to the surviving co-holder, not to his heirs. But like a tenancy in common, either joint tenant can sell or transfer his/her share of the property at any time, without the consent of the other. In fact, the only difference between the two is that joint tenancy avoids probate and automatic equal shares; tenancy in common passes through probate and the shares are not automatically equal.

Advantages

- In case of a divorce, both owners get their share.
- When one owner dies his share goes directly to the surviving co-holder and generally avoids probate and possible challenges by heirs.

Disadvantages

- Either owner can unilaterally convert the joint tenancy to tenants in common by selling or giving away his share.
- Creditors (including an ex-spouse) can place a lien on the property. You will be unable to sell or refinance without paying off the lien.
- Persistent creditors will be able to force a sale.

- When one spouse dies, one-half the value of the property will be subject to federal and maybe state death tax.

Joint tenants by the entirety

"JOHN AND MARY SMITH as tenants by the entirety," is the way this form of ownership reads. This is a special type of joint tenancy available only to married couples. Unlike regular joint tenancy, two signatures are required to transfer ownership. Only about half of the states recognize this form of ownership, but where it is available it provides special protection. In some states, Pennsylvania for example, it offers absolute protection against creditors taking the home. It is often used when one spouse is particularly at risk for lawsuits (a business owner, for example).

Advantages

- Unlike joint tenancy, in most states that recognize tenancy by the entirety your creditors other than the tax authorities cannot attach or force a sale of the property unless both spouses are liable on the debt.
- If your spouse owes money, his creditors generally cannot place a lien on the property while you are

alive. Even with a lien, creditors would not be able to force a sale. (If the non-debtor spouse were to die first, however, the debtor spouse would own the property alone and his creditors could go after it.)

- If the debtor spouse dies first, his debt will be extinguished and the non-debtor will not be liable. (Lenders try to get around this built-in consumer protection by demanding both spouses' signatures on debts.)
- When one owner dies, the property passes directly to the survivor and avoids probate and possible challenges by heirs.

Disadvantages

- If you own a house and decide to hold it this way with your spouse to protect you from lawsuits, you give away one-half ownership that can't unilaterally be taken back.
- If either of you owes money and you were to get a divorce, sell the property, or move to another home, creditors could move in immediately.

Q. So how should you hold your house?
A. It depends on your goals.

AS YOU SEE, NO MATTER how you hold a home with your new spouse, in one way or another it is still vulnerable.

- If you want to ***gain protection from your spouse's creditors or possible lawsuits*** (business-related, accidents, etc.), hold it as tenants by the entirety.

If you are quite certain that there are no old creditors lurking in the background you may be more interested in the estate planning aspects of title designation than in protection. In that case here are your choices:

- If you want to ***make sure the house goes directly to your spouse when you die*** with no possibility of anybody else claiming a piece, hold it as tenants by the entirety.
- If you want to ***make sure half your house goes to your children when you die,*** not your spouse, hold it as tenants in common (though it will then pass through probate and be vulnerable to a claim by the surviving spouse.)
- If you ***want to gain some protection from your spouse's creditors or possible lawsuits*** (business

related, accidents, etc.), hold it as tenants by the entirety.

If you want to accomplish these protections and take maximum advantage of significant tax savings when you die, there is another alternative: Set up a trust (see Chapters 6 and 13).

Declaration of Homestead, the homeowner's friend

THERE'S SOMETHING ELSE you can do to protect your house from creditors: "homestead" your property. This is a simple legal procedure that allows you, as head of the household, to protect your home from being taken in a lawsuit. If either spouse owns a high risk business you should not miss out on this protection.

Most states have some kind of homestead exemption, but the rules vary widely in how much equity can be protected. In New York, $10,000 is protected; in California, $75,000; in Massachusetts, $100,000; in Texas and Florida it's the entire amount.

Filing a declaration of homestead will not protect your property from a judgment if you owe back taxes, either federal or state, mortgage payments, delinquent alimony or child support. In some states it will not protect you from debts incurred before you bought the property.

C H A P T E R 6

USING A TRUST TO PROTECT YOUR ASSETS

We've just looked at the ways you can "hold" your assets and house to protect them from various threats that could arise when you remarry. There's another way that you can protect them that offers a number of other side benefits as well. You can put your assets and/or your house in a trust.

What is a trust?

A TRUST IS A LEGAL instrument established by you for the purpose of holding a house, savings account, investments, vacation property or any other asset that you want to place in it. The trust literally owns the assets, not you. Assets are held for someone's benefit (the beneficiary) and controlled by someone called a trustee.

It is a ***revocable trust*** if the person who establishes it (typically called the settlor, donor or grantor if real estate) maintains full control including the right to modify or terminate the instrument at any time. It is an irrevocable trust if these rights are given up. Revocable, or irrevocable, they are called ***living trusts*** when they take effect while you are alive.

You can put one in your will to go into effect after you die. This is called a ***testamentary trust*** and is always irrevocable. These trusts, however, do not avoid probate with all the possibility for challenges and legal fees it entails.

All trusts have on thing in common: you can hold assets under whatever terms you dictate. Living trusts are becoming increasingly popular because they can serve so many purposes. A trust can protect your assets in case you divorce, protect your estate from creditors, help you avoid death taxes, and even act as a will. You can instruct the trustee to do anything you want with your assets either during your life, after you die (including holding them for other generations), or both. Let's look at some of the options available with a trust.

Prenuptial planning

A REVOCABLE LIVING TRUST is an excellent way to keep your assets separate when you remarry. If set up in conjunction with a prenuptial agreement, assets placed in the trust are owned by the trust and do not get tagged as marital property during the marriage, even in community property states.

WARNING A trust set up without a premarital agreement may offer little or no protection because a divorce court could consider assets in the trust marital property subject to division. The premarital agreement must meet all the criteria we discussed earlier — full disclosure, fairness, no pressure and representation on both sides (see Chapter 2). Your spouse's signature on the agreement shows that you did not use the trust to fraudulently transfer your assets out of your spouse's reach.

Protection from creditors

IF YOUR SPOUSE HAS PROBLEMS with creditors, an ex or the IRS, a trust can offer you an extra measure of protection. Assets placed in the trust before your marriage are clearly not owned jointly with your spouse. Your spouse's creditors have no claim on them although your own creditors might be able to go after them.

Estate planning

IF THE GOAL IS TO TO ADD estate planning to protection, both spouses can set up trusts to hold their assets and pass them on to their respective children when they die. One of the best uses of this instrument is to hold your house for use by you and your spouse and then pass it to your children after your death.

WARNING If your purpose in setting up a trust is to keep your assets separate in case of a divorce, don't place in it property you acquire together during your marriage. And don't use joint funds to pay for assets in the trust—to make mortgage payments on a house, for instance. To do so could undermine the very thing you were trying to accomplish: separation.

Revocable living trusts

AS THE GRANTOR OF A revocable living trust you retain full control; you can even be the trustee. If you put your house in the trust, you can still sell, rent, or refinance it. When you remarry, a trust allows you to do some interesting things with your home. You can make your spouse the beneficiary and allow him to live in your house after you die provided he fulfills certain obligations and/or abides by restrictions you build into the trust. For instance, you could permit him to reside there provided that he cares for your twelve cats and doesn't remarry.

The trust can even act as your will passing the property to your children when he dies. The trust clearly spells out who can only use your house and who will ultimately own it. Here's an example of how a trust can be used to accomplish several goals:

Ruth is a businesswoman who owns her own home, which she purchased for $50,000 and now is worth $150,000. She has two grown sons.

Ruth marries John who has two grown daughters and alimony obligations. She wants to be sure that if she dies before John, he will have a home for the rest of his life and her sons will get the house when John passes away.

In addition, Ruth doesn't want certain people to be able to get their hands on her property. Specifically, John has disgruntled cred-

itors from a bad business investment and his ex is constantly after him for more money. Her accountant points out that even if she cuts him out of her will completely, he could demand and get his statutory share (see Chapter 13) and her money would then be fair prey for his creditors. The accountant has a better idea.

Ruth establishes the Ruth Newton Revocable Trust under these terms:

- Ruth is the grantor and trustee.
- As grantor, she maintains the right to receive any benefits of the property while she is alive, including the right to live there and collect rent from the basement apartment, and to sell or refinance it if she wishes.
- John is the beneficiary with the right to continue living in the house after her death as long as he does not remarry.
- When John no longer needs it, the property goes directly to her sons, bypassing his estate, his ex-wife, his creditors and his children.

Tax advantages

LIVING TRUSTS OFFER an opportunity for very effective estate planning. Besides protecting her house, the trust allows Ruth's estate to realize some tidy tax savings.

Ruth's children probably will sell the house after John's death and a capital gains tax may be due. Here's how that works:

The taxable gain is determined by taking the purchase price of the asset, plus the cost of major improvements and deducting the total from the sale price. In this case Ruth paid $50,000 for the house. This is called her cost basis (she did not do any major improvements). If she were to sell it for $150,000, her capital gain would be $100,000.

Ruth considered making an outright gift of the house to her kids. Her accountant explained that she would be "gifting" them her basis ($50,000), therefore they would have a substantial capital gain and a big tax bill — 27 percent or more.

Her accountant explained that it would be better from a tax perspective for her children to inherit the house. If Ruth dies with the house in her name, it will go through her taxable estate to her children. The current value of the house (*not* what she actually paid for it) as listed on the death tax return becomes her children's new "stepped up basis". But what about state and federal death tax?

Good news: Under the law, tax is due only on estates worth more than $600,000. In Ruth's case there would be a very small tax. She decides that it makes good tax sense to have the property go through her taxable estate to give her children a "stepped up basis".

Although this option seems attractive from a tax point of view, Ruth does not want to have her property go through probate. She knows that probate is a public process which allows anybody with a cause to claim a piece of her estate. She doesn't want her husband, his ex, or his creditors to be able to get a share.

Ruth solves the problem by establishing a revocable living trust. The house is owned by the trust and therefore does not go through probate. And since she had full control over the assets in her trust while she was alive, it is part of her taxable estate when she dies.

Here's what will happen when Ruth passes away. Her children will file a death tax return for their mother. The basis at the time gets "stepped-up" to the house's fair market value ($150,000). The only tax that may be due is a state death tax. But even so it's certain to be less than the capital gains rate her children would have paid had she just given them the house. If they were to sell it right then and there, there would be no capital gains tax due.

However, the way Ruth sets it up, the house cannot be sold until John dies because he has lifetime use of the house. The only gain will be any appreciation over the new basis ($150,000) during the time between Ruth's death and John's.

Advantages

There are some obvious advantages to using a revocable living trust. You may be thinking that one of these could work well for you. Here's a recap of the features of a revocable living trust that you might find attractive:

- A revocable trust set up before your marriage is an effective way to keep your assets separate and protect them in case of a divorce.
- Property in the trust bypasses probate. Therefore there is little possibility that anyone including your children will be able to challenge your wishes after you die.
- By avoiding probate, no one knows your financial business.
- Revocable trusts are tax neutral meaning that you can still deduct real estate taxes on your return. If the property is sold after you turn 55, you still keep the one-time $125,000 capital gain exemption. And the ultimate heirs after your spouse dies (typically your children) get a "stepped up" basis when they eventually sell it.

- If you alone set up the trust, your spouse's ex cannot reach the assets. Even if you make him a beneficiary with instructions that he be allowed to continue to enjoy the benefits of the assets after your death, his ex could not reach them.
- Your assets are safe from your spouse's creditors. Your spouse, as a beneficiary, doesn't own the assets, only the right to enjoy them.

Disadvantages

- Your spouse's creditors are blocked, but your creditors, if they try hard enough, could probably reach the assets during your lifetime and maybe even after you die.
- Other than the possibility of getting a stepped up basis at the time of death, a revocable trust offers no favorable tax consequences. In other words you continue to pay tax on income generated from the trust. In addition, assets in the trust are subject to death (inheritance) taxes after both spouses die. Capital gains and gift taxes are also applicable just as if you owned the assets directly.
- If you get a divorce a revocable trust set up after the marriage offers no guarantee of protection. Because

you maintain full control over the assets, a court could well consider them marital property.

- If your spouse's ex is trying to get money, he could be ordered to pay more on the grounds that as beneficiary of your assets he has more funds available.

Irrevocable trusts

AN IRREVOCABLE TRUST, as the name implies, is carved in stone. There may be times when that feature makes it an attractive option. For instance, suppose Ruth owns a successful catering business. She worries that if one of her customers chokes on a fish bone she might get sued. She considers putting her assets in an irrevocable trust with herself as beneficiary and a friend or relative as trustee. She would derive the same benefits as with a revocable trust, but she'd pay a higher price for them. Here's why:

The trouble with an irrevocable trust is that the donor (in this case, Ruth) surrenders control of the assets to the trustee. And although she'd never be able to get her assets back, other people might still be able to get them. Her customer who choked on a fish bone probably could not get her assets providing the trust was set up before the accident and not after as a way of evading a judgment. But suppose she sets up the trust after her marriage to John and the marriage doesn't last. A divorce court might consider the trust a fraudulent conveyance for the purpose of depriving John of his rightful share of their marital property. If that happens, the trust would be broken.

There are certainly times when an irrevocable trust is useful or even necessary. For example, if one spouse were to need long-term care in a nursing home, an irrevocable trust can be an absolute lifesaver (see Chapter 12). Under less dire circumstances, however, most people are not willing to give up complete control of their assets.

CHAPTER 7

TAXES: HE, SHE, & UNCLE SAM MAKES THREE

Several years ago, federal tax laws favored single people. If you were unmarried on December 31, then "single" was your filing status for the whole year, even if you had been married for the other 364 days. Some people flew to a tropical resort each December to get a divorce. They filed their tax returns as single people, saved the cost of their vacation in taxes, even pocketed several thousand dollars, and remarried in January of the following year. Then they got divorced again in 11 months. The IRS now regards antics like these as fraudulent. But the question is moot really, because the Tax Reform Act of 1986 pretty much eliminated the big tax advantages for single people.

Single or married — Any tax savings?

TODAY IF YOU ARE wondering how matrimony will affect your tax situation, the answer is probably "not much." The maximum saving now available for an unmarried couple each earning $50,000 would be $1,300. If they were to get married the lost tax saving might easily be offset by other factors.

From a tax perspective, then, it doesn't much matter whether you remain single or get married. Once you do decide to marry, however, your first concern is, Should you file individually (called "married filing separately") or jointly?

This issue will come up within your first year of wedlock so be prepared. The logic behind filing jointly is this: If one partner has significantly less taxable income and therefore a lower tax rate than the other, a joint filing can reap a small saving. Where income is low, this option may be attractive.

But effectively this advantage disappears if the couple has combined taxable income of about $40,000 or more. Beyond that, from a tax-saving standpoint it makes little difference whether you file jointly or separately.

From a risk standpoint, however, there can be a big difference. In fact, many tax preparers advise people who bring assets to a marriage to use the "married-filing-separately" format to protect each of them from unexpected tax liabilities.

The Perils of Joint Filing

DO YOU REALIZE THAT your signature on your joint tax return exposes you to serious consequences should the IRS challenge the validity of your spouse's reporting? The IRS can go back to challenge any return filed within the past three years. Once you sign a joint return, you assume responsibility for the accuracy of all the information on that document, not just your portion.

The IRS will hold you equally liable if your spouse has under-reported income or claimed unjustified deductions. You may be able to demonstrate that you were an "innocent spouse" (that you had no knowledge of the irregularities). If you can't, you and your spouse probably will face additional taxes, plus penalties and interest.

If the amount of the discrepancy is less than 20 percent the IRS tends to see it as an honest error and the statue of limitations is therefore three years. But the IRS automatically regards amounts over 20 percent as possible fraud. Where fraud is suspected, the statute of limitations is six years.

It's not always easy to prove that you were an "innocent spouse". If your husband bought a yacht and you knew he couldn't afford it on the income he claimed, the IRS will take the position that you should have known something was amiss.

However, the IRS can be persuaded by certain facts and conditions. Suppose your mate kept the boat in the

Caribbean and you knew nothing about it, never benefited from it, never saw his checkbook or bills, and, in fact, never were involved in any of his financial matters. You'd probably be able to convince them that you should not be penalized. Filing separately, however, relieves you of the possibility of becoming enmeshed in this kind of sticky situation.

By the way, if you filed jointly with your ex-spouse and he later develops tax problems, the IRS can come after you and whatever assets you hold with your new spouse years later. Things can get out of hand even if nobody ever meant to do anything sneaky. Here's a true story (names changed) that illustrates "innocent" liability.

The capital gain boomerang

JOE AND FRAN HAD WHAT is known as an amicable divorce in 1988 and split their assets 50-50. They each pocketed half the proceeds of the sale of their house before the divorce was finalized. Under the law, if each reinvested the money in a home of equal or greater value within two years, neither would owe tax on the capital gain. If one or the other did not buy a home, in their divorce agreement they each assumed responsibility for the taxes owed on their portion. All the negotiations were characterized by civility and cooperation. They filed their last joint tax return and divorced in March.

Fran quickly married a man named Harry and reinvested her share of the proceeds in their new home thereby eliminating her tax liability. Joe looked at houses but never closed on one. Then he ran into a period of bad luck. He made some bad investments, lost his job and had to use the rest of his share to live on. Four years later, Fran got a letter from the IRS telling her she owed over $50,000 in back taxes for Joe's portion of the liability.

She argued that the statute of limitations had run out. The IRS countered that their tax return for 1988 was technically never closed since Joe had not gone back to amend it to show that he had not reinvested the money as he intended.

Moreover, the IRS didn't care what the divorce agreement said; her signature was on their joint tax return, and Fran was liable for the full amount if Joe defaulted. Joe was now doing just that because he had no assets and was flat broke.

Again Fran tried to persuade the IRS to reconsider. She argued that she believed that Joe had reinvested the money in a house and therefore she was an innocent spouse. The IRS, however, was unmoved. Fran should have known, they argued, that she was assuming responsibility for the possible tax liability when she signed the return. Case closed. The newlyweds faced a lien on their new home if they didn't pay Joe's bill.

All of these headaches would have been avoided if Fran and Joe had filed separately.

Fraud victim takes double blow

SOMETIMES THERE CAN BE fraud involved but not by either spouse. Here's another true story (names changed) to illustrate the chilling long-term effects of filing jointly.

Through a trusted friend Harvey heard about a great tax shelter: a mink farm in Denmark. He invested $100,000 and became a partner in the farm. The money went to a promoter in New Jersey and Harvey received financial statements from the farm in Denmark showing losses that he then deducted from his tax liability. Harvey's wife Doreen knew little about the scheme.

Three years into the venture Doreen divorced Harvey and remarried. She and her new husband were living a tranquil life when one day she got a letter from the IRS. It seems Harvey had claimed losses from his mink farm investment on a recent tax return. The losses were so substantial that the IRS got curious. After a little snooping they smelled a rat in the mink pen. They investigated documents from the agent in New Jersey and the Danish enterprise. They found checks from the "mink farm" to phony accounts for the purchase of mink herds and checks from the broker to the mink farm when the animals were "sold". Although several business entities were involved, each with its own stationery, bank accounts and invoices, when investigators studied the type on all the documents they found that it came from the same typewriter. They tracked the typewriter to the pro-

moter's basement in Brooklyn. The mink farm was but a figment of his nefarious imagination!

Harvey was astounded. He had been duped by a smooth-talking con artist. Unfortunately, he now owed $175,000 in back taxes, interest and penalties. Since her signature was on their joint return, Doreen and all her assets were on the hook too!

This story took place before Congress changed the tax code in 1986. Prior to that time, losses from passive investments like a mink farm or real estate could be used to offset ordinary income like salary and wages. After 1986, losses from passive income could only be applied to other passive activity. Although this change made certain kinds of tax shelters less attractive, a situation like the above could still crop up today. Again, filing separately precludes this kind of headache.

Keeping your refund in your pocket

THE IRS FROWNS ON PARENTS who fall behind in their child support payments and assists custodial parents to collect by allowing them to intercept federal and state tax refunds. If your current spouse is delinquent and you have filed jointly, *your* refund may be snagged with your spouse's. In this situation, you are what is known as an "Injured Spouse" in IRS parlance.

Here's a tip: You can get your piece of the check separated out by filing a claim with the IRS on a special form. To get a copy, call 1 800 TAX-FORM and ask for the Injured Spouse Claim and Allocation Form, #8379.

If the Injured Spouse's residence was in a community property state (see Chapter 3) refunds must be divided according to state law, not according to who earned them. Instructions on the form state, "Generally, claims from [community property states] California, Idaho, Louisiana, and Texas will result in no refund for the injured spouse."

If your spouse is receiving Social Security, these checks may also be garnished to satisfy support obligations to a former wife or children.

I have an IRA account. Will my remarriage affect it?

YES IT WILL. AND THE LAW may seem quite unfair.

Debra, twice divorced, was determined to look after herself financially. When she was single, she began faithfully to deposit money into her IRA every year. After some years, she married a man who had a pension through his company. Under the law, she was no longer allowed to deduct her IRA contributions on her tax return. A few years after their marriage, her husband's employer filed for bank-

ruptcy. His pension was cut drastically and the spousal benefits were decimated. Yet Debra still could not make deposits into her IRA account without paying taxes on the money.

This is one case where the tax law discriminates against married people. If you are covered under your spouse's pension plan, even if only minimally, your IRA contribution loses its tax-exempt status.

My husband is withholding alimony payments because his ex has not returned property that belongs to him, but he's deducting them on our tax return. He'll pay her when she turns over the property. Can he get into trouble for doing this?

NOT ONLY CAN HE GET into trouble, you can too. Alimony is tax deductible to the payer and subject to taxation as income to the recipient. If your husband has been deducting the alimony on his tax return and you sign jointly, the IRS can go after back tax, penalties and interest from both of you.

WARNING If you ever consider doing something a little "irregular" on your taxes remember this: The IRS receives more tipoffs from disgruntled wives than any other source.

CHAPTER 8

REMARRIAGE AND CHILDREN: YOURS, MINE & OURS

Experts say it costs a quarter of a million dollars to raise a child to adulthood. That's just cash. What about the value of non-monetary services like child care and associated housework? Studies estimate that adds another $125,000. Tack on the possibility of advanced education and you could reach half a million dollars before one baby bird leaves the nest!

MANAGING MONEY IS NOT EASY when there are children involved. Not only are finances more complicated in combined families, statistics tell us there is less money to go around. The man may be trying to build a new life with a new wife and baby while obligations to his old family siphon his bank account. The former wife feels she is barely getting by; the new wife complains that she and her children are taking a back seat to his former family.

Your husband's obligation to support his children from a former marriage (change the gender and the discussion still applies)

IT IS IMPORTANT THAT you both understand what your spouse's continuing obligation will be after remarriage. Clearly he is not going to be able to reduce his support payments just because he's marrying you. And there is no court that will obligate you to pay support for his children while they are living with his ex-wife. Don't think, however, that courts haven't indirectly made spouses of later marriages pay child support for their stepchildren. Here's how *that* works:

Sally and Ted plan to marry. Ted has three young children who live with his ex-wife. Ted's income is $750 per week; he is paying

$200 of it in child support. Sally earns $500 a week. They put together a prenuptial agreement that states among other things that neither party is responsible for the other's preexisting debts or obligations. Two years later Ted's ex decides to seek increased child support.

In court, Ted's financial statement shows that his salary has barely increased over the past five years. His ex-wife's lawyer argues that although Ted's present wife has no obligation to pay for Ted's children, she is contributing to the couple's joint obligations. Ted, therefore, has more money free to pay support. The court accepts the mother's argument and increases Ted's support payment by $50 a week.

This story is repeated over and over again all across the country. Second spouses are not insulated from having their paychecks go, albeit indirectly, for the support of someone else's children. Marital contracts offer little protection because the courts always put the welfare of the children above all else.

Your spouse's ex-wife is getting remarried. Will his support obligations be reduced?

HAVING READ THE PREVIOUS example, you would expect that the answer would be yes. Guess again! True, her new husband will be contributing to her household expenses, as in the previous case. So it would make sense that your husband's obligation would be reduced.

But it usually doesn't happen that way. The minute your husband and his ex-wife go into court for a modification two arguments arise:

1) His ex-wife might concede that her new husband is helping out with some expenses but she'll claim that the childrens' expenses have gone up even more over the years for which she has not been reimbursed.

2) Guess whose financial statement the ex-wife wants to see. If you said her former husband's, you're only half right. She'll want to see yours as well and will argue that her former husband's expenses have been substantially reduced by your income. And she also will point out that the two of you don't have the day to day expenses of rearing the children.

WARNING Do not go into a marriage thinking that you will be immune from having to contribute to the support of someone else's children. And don't expect that your husband's financial obligation will be reduced if his former wife remarries. Chances are that just the opposite will happen.

Your spouse's ex is living with her boyfriend. Does that affect his support obligations?

IN SOME STATES, CO-HABITATION automatically terminates alimony. In many states, your spouse might be able to have alimony reduced or eliminated if he can show that his ex's financial circumstances have materially improved since her lover moved in. But if her boyfriend is an unemployed butterfly-catcher who doesn't contribute to the household expenses, forget it.

The possibility of having your husband's child support obligations reduced because his ex-wife is now living with someone is more remote than if she actually married her new friend. And remember the chances of that happening aren't great.

The problem is especially difficult because it's hard to pin down whether or not they are actually living together. If he is asked, dollars to doughnuts the boyfriend will say: "I just visit there occasionally. Really, I'm living with my mother." What's more you're not going to find joint checking accounts or monthly bills in both party's names. The most the ex-wife will admit is, "Once in a while he gives me a couple of dollars to help me out because their father was late with his child support payment."

By the way, you would only get all this useless information about her finances after you spent $3,000 to $5,000 in legal fees!

If you are considering going to court for a modification of your support obligations, consider the legal expenses. For instance:

Sandra's lawyer was furious. Sandra's husband was dragging her into court to try to get a reduction of his child support. His case was being handled by two attorneys from the biggest law firm in the city. He spent more on them than he would on just paying the disputed amount for the next four years. Not to mention his wife's legal bills. All the money that should have gone toward the children's needs went into the pockets of lawyers.

WARNING Nine times out of ten the modification will cost you more in legal fees than you could save in support payments. Forget it. Don't hire a lawyer. Send your support payments according to your agreement and remember the important thing is the welfare of your children.

My ex is always trying to get more money. Will she be able to do it?

IN THE BEST OF DIVORCES both parties are equally unhappy with the outcome. Given this as your starting point is it any wonder that one or the other may try to improve the deal? When the mother feels that she is carrying too much of the load she may go back to court to seek higher child support. Sometimes the increase is justified because the children's needs are not being met. But sometimes support issues can become a vendetta to even the score. Or the mother may not have a realistic view of what her ex-husband is able to afford.

WARNING Fathers: If you honestly believe that you should not be made to pay more support, there are some things you can do to protect yourself. Keep records of all payments that are above the monthly check. There may be large items like camp or medical expenses, or numerous small ones that add up — clothes, spending money, special treats. (Well worth spending extra on is health insurance for the child if the custodial spouse does not have it.)

To receive an increase the custodial parent must prove that the non-custodial parent's financial circumstances have improved *materially* in ways not anticipated at the time of the divorce. As noted, your new spouse's contribution to household expenses will undoubtedly become an issue. Don't brag about money in front of your kids. Stories can go back to your ex-wife that may lead to misunderstandings or worse.

My ex-wife is using my support payments for her deadbeat boyfriend. Do I still have to pay?

THE FOLLOWING EXAMPLE contains an issue that many people don't understand: the issue of, Do I still have to send child support to my ex when it benefits her boyfriend?

Mario's ex wife is living with Gerard, an unemployed actor. Mario's blood pressure goes through the roof when he picks up his kids and sees Gerard pulling out of the driveway in the car Mario pays for or lounging around on Mario's former patio. Mario tells his ex, "If you don't get rid of that ☆#☆#, I'm not sending you any more child support checks."

With the Family Support Act of 1988 federal laws governing child support have become tougher. No matter how angry you are at the situation, do not give in to the temptation to withhold child support payments. Refusal to pay child support when you are financially able to do so is a crime in all states. It's also unfair to your children. If you see signs that the money is not being used for the children, however, such as shabby clothes or health problems unattended, you can ask the court to allow you to pay the childrens' bills directly.

WARNING The federal government and the states have stiffened their collection procedures and you could face wage attachments, some very unpleasant moments in court, or even time in jail.

Just remember, hurting your ex-wife probably will hurt your children too.

Your ex sabotages your visits with your kids. Do you still have to pay support?

OCCASIONALLY THE COURTS WILL stop child support when visitation orders are consistently violated, but never if there will be a negative impact on the welfare of the child.

A message to ex-wives who withhold visitations to punish their former husbands: Several studies have demonstrated that fathers who are able to maintain a close relationship with their children are more likely to keep up with their child support payments. Aside from the detrimental effect parental hostilities can have on children, from a financial standpoint it's poor policy. Wives who turn their children against their father lay the foundation for retaliation not to mention the psychological damage to the children.

WARNING Mothers: Try to keep your angry feelings from interfering with your children's relationship with their father. He may have been a crummy husband, but he might be a pretty good dad. At any rate, he's a part of your children's emotional network. And you could be causing worse problems. Interfering in their relationship may have the side effect of depriving your children financially.

You have married someone who has custody of children from a previous marriage. At some point will you wind up having to support your stepchildren?

COMBINED FAMILIES WITH children from two or more marriages have to deal with bills, bills and more bills — uninsured medical expenses like the dentist, braces, and glasses—summer camp, uniforms and equipment for sports, instruments for school band, class trips, piano lessons, gymnastics. What if there is a major illness, mental or physical? Or an injury? What about indirect expenses — a child wrecks the family car or hits a baseball through the neighbor's plate glass window? Can these things affect you as a stepparent?

Under common law, every one of these bills is the sole responsibility of the biological parents. Stepparents cannot be held legally responsible for any of them.

That said, however, like everything else with the law, there are exceptions. Let's look at two similar situations with very different implications.

In loco parenti: a voluntarily-assumed obligation.

MILLIONS OF STEPPARENTS voluntarily provide financial assistance and even total support for their stepchildren. They do it for many reasons: out of love for the children's parent or for the children themselves, out of a sense of duty and compassion, or because the biological parent can't or won't do it. Whatever the reason, millions of stepparents pour out billions of dollars for children they are not legally required to support.

This behavior places them in a specific position in the eyes of the law. They are acting *in loco parenti* (in place of the parent) in whole or in part. Here's an example:

Bill marries Barbara who has a son, Timmy (age 2). Because Bill takes care of Timmy and assumes financial responsibility for him, the law recognizes that he is acting in loco parenti, *he "stands in place of" Timmy's biological father. Should Bill wish to be reimbursed by the natural father, a court will recognize his rights. But if he and the child's mother later divorce, he will not be obliged to continue supporting Timmy since the* in loco parenti *relationship is entirely voluntary on the part of the stepparent and can be terminated at will.*

The law was designed this way so that stepparents would not be afraid to help out with their stepchild lest they be on the hook forever. The only time a stepparent acting *in loco parenti* might be obliged to pay is in a dire emergency where the child has no other support and may become a public charge. The welfare department can then bring an action against the stepparent on behalf of the child.

The estoppel doctrine: an involuntary obligation

HERE'S ANOTHER scenario.

Timmy's natural father offers to pay for the child's support but stepfather Bill refuses. He doesn't like the man and doesn't want him around. In fact, Bill actively discourages Timmy's father from even seeing the boy.

Bill is crazy about Timmy and refers to him as "my son." Timmy calls him "Daddy" and refers to Bill's parents as Grandma and Grandpa. Bill claims the child as a dependent on his tax returns, and even offers to adopt him. Although the adoption never goes through,

Timmy uses his stepfather's last name and it appears on all his school records.

But the marriage does not work out. Bill and Barbara file for divorce and Bill claims that he had been acting in loco parenti. *Since legally this is a voluntary relationship, his support obligations to Timmy can terminate at will, specifically at the time of the divorce.*

When the case gets to court, however, the judge disagrees. He cites the doctrine of "equitable estoppel". That means that although a stepparent has no legal obligation to support a child, he may on the basis of fairness *incur that responsibility when the following conditions occur:*

- **Representation** The stepparent offers himself as the child's parent including providing financial support.
- **Detriment** The stepparent interferes with the child's relationship with the natural parent and irretrievably blocks financial support from that parent.
- **Reliance** The child relies upon the love and financial support of the stepparent.

The estoppel doctrine is based on fairness. When these three conditions exist a court may rule that *in fairness* to the child the stepparent is prohibited from denying support.

The court notes that Bill strongly encouraged Timmy to regard him as his father and that Timmy had relied on the love and financial support of his stepfather as if he were his natural parent. The close bond between Bill and Timmy would not alone have been enough to invoke the estoppel doctrine. But Bill had gone further by driving away Timmy's natural father. With his father gone, if Bill's love and financial support were withdrawn, the court held that Timmy would have been irreparably harmed. Bill was ordered to continue to support Timmy.

Today's courts more and more tend to view these situations from the perspective of, What's in the best interest of the child? On the other hand, courts recognize that they must not in effect penalize stepparents who love and help their stepchildren while rewarding those who remain aloof. This expanded view of stepparents' obligations blurs the distinctions that once clearly limited the stepparent's role. The point is not that you should withhold support and care from your stepchildren. Unless there is very good reason, however, think twice before you stand between the child and his biological parent.

WARNING You will never get into trouble by loving your stepchild. It is a potential problem only at the point where you aggressively interfere with the child's relationship with his biological parent and develop a pattern of paying for a child's necessary expenses when the natural parent would be willing to do it.

College tuition — who pays?

THAT'S A QUESTION the courts are dealing with more and more these days as they attempt to tie up the loose strings from divorces of a decade or so ago. Divorce agreements then often dealt with the issue of college in vague terms: "Each parent will be responsible for college costs in proportion to his/her ability to pay", was typical. That seemed adequate during the 80s because the economy was booming and both parents probably assumed that college costs would be manageable when the time came. Today, with new spouses and maybe additional children, many parents faced with escalating college costs are finding that they are now unable to contribute adequately.

Can an ex-spouse be forced to pay for a child's college education?

WHAT HAPPENS WHEN the mother of a brilliant child saves money to pay her half of college costs and the father can't pay his share? Can the court order that the kid must attend a state school rather than place a financial burden on the unprepared parent? Even if it means giving up Harvard? Can the court order the father to get a loan? Can it order the parent of a C student to take out a loan?

There are few answers because this area of the law is still relatively undefined. But as college tuitions soar and incomes sag under the weight of a sluggish economy, many former spouses are finding themselves back in court fighting over the issue of what each is obliged to contribute to the education of their children.

Can a stepparent be forced to pay for a child's college education?

THE ISSUE GETS EVEN MORE complicated when one or the other parent has remarried:

Patricia marries Sam who has one child, Tommy, of college age. His divorce agreement obligates him and his ex-wife Denise to contribute equally to their child's college education subject to their financial resources. At the time of the divorce they both had approximately the same income.

Tommy starts college and his parents each contribute $9,000 for the first year. Denise gets laid off from her job and now requests that Sam pay more than half of the expenses. He says he can't afford to do it. Pat sits on the sidelines figuring that whatever happens she's not going to be affected.

True, Pat has absolutely no legal obligation to contribute to Tommy's college education. True, the divorce agreement states that the biological parents will contribute equally subject to their financial resources. And true, his income has not gone up over the past few years. So Pat is in the clear, right? Guess again.

As we've seen, a court cannot order a stepparent to pay for stepchildren, but it will take into consideration all resources available to the parent who is obligated to pay support. It would be impossible for Pat to argue that her contributing to the household expenses does not free up Sam's money to use for Tommy's college tuition. What happens if the court rules that Sam has to pay more? Sam's money will go toward tuition and Pat will have to pick up more of their living expenses.

How to even the score

PRACTICALLY SPEAKING, there is no way to preclude this scenario. However, if Pat has a child there may be a way to offset the money she indirectly contributes to Tommy's education. For instance:

Pat has a teenage daughter, Sara, who will be starting college in three years. In a premarital agreement she makes a provision that Sam will be obligated to pay toward her daughter's college bill an amount equal to the additional living expenses Pat assumes.

But Pat's ex-husband is wealthy and is willing to assume all of Sara's tuition costs. Sam doesn't believe that he should have to con-

tribute to Sara's education since her biological father can carry it. Pat feels she is subsidizing Tommy's education at her own child's expense. She may want Sam to put an equal amount into a trust fund for Sara. After all, even if Sara doesn't need it for college, it would be there for her wedding or as a down payment on a house.

This is the kind of unanticipated question that could be resolved in a postmarital agreement (see Chapter 2). If the marriage ends, daughter Sara's interests are still protected.

Will your remarriage affect your child's financial aid?

QUITE LIKELY. COLLEGE AID offices always ask to see the financial statement of the custodial parent. If that parent has remarried, they will ask to see the new spouse's financials too, even though they know the new spouse has no legal obligation to contribute to the stepchild's education. They regard the stepparent's income as part of the total picture.

If the child is "emancipated" (legal age varies state by state from 18 to 21), he can apply for financial aid on his own. However, if you provided more than half of his support or claimed him as a dependent within the last two years, the college will look to you to pay.

Can a prenuptial agreement shield the stepparent's income from the college?

When Chloe's son Philip went off to college he was able to qualify for $8,000 a year in financial aid based on his mother's limited income and assets. Chloe remarried during Philip's sophomore year. She and her new husband drew up a prenuptial agreement separating their assets and liabilities. Nevertheless to the couple's dismay, Philip lost his scholarships because the family's income was now considered too high. Chloe had to foot the bill.

Most schools ask for financial information from the non-custodial parent. If he or she is unwilling to provide it there's not much they can do other than to withhold aid which, of course, puts the child on the spot. The parent who is most active in helping the child get an education will then bear the scrutiny and the burden for payment, whatever the college decides. A prenuptial agreement probably will not help.

WARNING When you remarry, your new spouse's assets and income could cause your child's financial aid to be reduced or lost.

Collecting child support — a national problem

IF YOU ARE HAVING TROUBLE collecting child support you are not alone. About half of those entitled to support receive only partial payments or none at all. The effect of non-payment of support on custodial parents (85 percent are women) can be devastating. Often the arrears mount to tens of thousands of dollars. When financially strapped custodial parents remarry, the repercussions spread to the next family.

In an effort to relieve this national problem, federal and state governments have toughened collection methods including allowing garnishment of wages and tax refunds, posting "wanted" posters of the delinquent parent in public places and imposing jail sentences. Still the problem involves 2.5 million non-paying parents and each agency has only a handful of workers handling a caseload of several hundred problem parents.

How to chase down back child support

YOUR FIRST OPTION IS to call the public agency that handles delinquent support cases. Their services are free. Look in the phone book under State Government, Social Services, Child Support Division; Federal

Office of Child Support Enforcement; your state Department of Revenue; or the district attorney's office. The court where you got your divorce can also refer you to the right agency.

Of course, dealing with a big bureaucracy is not easy. Once you reach the right person, you may get sympathy but help is another matter. These agencies have the means to garnish wages and intercept tax refunds but most are so overburdened and their resources so limited that their success rate is less than 20 percent.

Building a relationship with one case worker and staying in touch may help but it will take a long time to see results, if you ever do. Even if you track down the delinquent parent, he may not have the money and few judges feel comfortable throwing a father in jail for being broke.

If you don't get satisfaction, try another tack: Hire a private attorney. This can be very effective. The lawyer can institute proceedings to have support payments deducted directly from the parent's paycheck. He or she can also keep the pressure on to collect arrears by threatening to petition the court to have the parent jailed.

Unfortunately, each effort costs money, so by the time you pay the legal bills, you may have little or nothing left for the kids. Also recognize that there are people who quit working just to avoid paying. It's the "cut off your nose to spite your face" syndrome. One father who had his own business and a six-figure income abandoned his business and moved into a renovated bus. The judge was not impressed and ordered him to pay up or go to jail.

If you are dealing with one of this type, you may worry about spending money to chase him. In some jurisdictions, court workers are sympathetic to parents who are trying to avoid giving whatever money they collect to their lawyer rather than the children. You will need persistence but you can do it yourself. Take your support order to the office of the court that issued it and ask for help in acting *pro se* (on your own behalf without an attorney) to collect the arrears or begin a contempt action. Don't try to do this by phone. Instead, go in during the slower part of the day (generally mid-morning and mid-afternoon) and find someone willing to take the time to show you the steps you need to take.

One other possibility: Consider a private collection service. Again, this option costs money but perhaps less than a lawyer and it may be more effective than trying to do it yourself. Good sources of referrals are the people you speak with while pursuing option one.

You can't get blood from a stone — the other side of the story

New federal child support guidelines have raised the average support payment per child in most states, but many experts feel that the increase still isn't enough to cover the real costs associated with being the custodial spouse. And yet the hard fact behind child support delinquencies is that many men are trapped and crushed under the weight of their financial obligations. They have lost access to their children yet their bank accounts are so strained that there's no possibility of more children with a new wife. This situation has been called a "check book vasectomy."

Wives always feel that they are getting the short end of the stick. But here's the view from the other side.

Eliot is divorced. He earns $75,000 a year. The state he lives in (Massachusetts) has adopted a formula that determines how much child support Eliot has to pay for his three kids. It comes to almost $9,000 per child, or $27,000 plus half of their uninsured medical expenses. In his tax bracket, the IRS and other payroll deductions take another $28,000. The best he'll get to keep of his $75,000 income is less than $20,000.

The truth is divorce is too expensive for most men. Our courts do not have a clear view of whether the adoption of stepchildren or fathering of new children may be sufficient cause to reduce support payments for children from a previous marriage. Men who hope to build a new life often face very rough going.

How can I set aside money for my children that my ex can't touch?

EVERY STATE HAS A PROVISION that allows children to own small amounts of money without the necessity of going to a probate court to establish a trust fund for a minor child (typically under age 18). These laws are generally referred to as the Uniform Gift to Minors Act. The idea is pretty simple: A parent sets up an account and places money in it for the child. The child's Social Security number goes on the account and interest up to $1,000 a year will be taxed at the child's rate, if under age 14. Any interest over $1,000 pays tax at the parents' rate.

Advantages

- Once the gift is made, it no longer belongs to the parent and therefore cannot be reached by either parent's creditors.
- Your ex can never reach these assets, unless of course she claimed that they were originally hers and she transferred them to you.

Disadvantages

- You lose total, complete, irrevocable control over the money once it is given away. Some people would like to believe that they can still take this money for their own purposes at any time. Forget it! Not only do you give up the right ever to get the money again, every state requires that the custodian (you) be able to provide a full accounting of what happens to the assets while they're under your control. At age 14, your child has the right to demand an accounting from you. Who would tell the kid to do that? Try your former spouse!
- When the child reaches the age of majority (usually 18 or 21) the trust must terminate and all funds be paid to him or her. You may hope that the money will go toward college expenses but you'll have no control over what the kid does with it.

WARNING: Moving money into a child's account is not a method to protect it from your creditors. Usually, any transactions made within a year of the start of a lawsuit are assumed to be fraudulent conveyances.

How to provide for a disabled child

IF YOU HAVE A CHILD with a physical or mental disability, you may want to take steps to provide for him at the time you remarry. The problem takes on immediacy because medical science has developed miracles which prolong the life of severely disabled children who, in the past, might not have made it into adulthood.

What can you do to provide for an incapacitated child when you are no longer around to do it?

A SPECIAL NEEDS TRUST (SNT), if drafted carefully, can provide financial security for your child's lifetime and assure that whatever benefits he is now getting from the government or state will not be terminated.

You can establish a SNT to take effect while you are alive (in which case it is called a living trust) or upon your death (a testamentary trust). It's purpose is to hold a sum of money to be used for your child during his lifetime specifically to supplement the child's other benefits received from the state or federal government such as SSI (supplemental security income) and Medicaid.

The tricky part is that if your child receives income or assets from the trust the wrong way these benefits can be either reduced or terminated. Public policy, both federal and state, does recognize that publicly-funded benefits are usually inadequate to provide for a child's care. Therefore SNTs are allowed but their terms must be strictly followed.

The laws governing these trusts are terribly tricky and they change constantly. When you set up the trust the appointed trustee should have wide discretion in distributing the funds.You must be careful not to restrict a trustee's ability to respond to a child's needs now or in the future. What the government may allow today may be disallowed tomorrow. The key rule to follow is that income and principal must be used to supplement public benefits not take their place. Easier said then done, however.

It is absolutely essential that your lawyer and trustee be fully aware of how the programs that your child receives benefits from operate. The following is an outline intended to help you understand how the system works and what's at risk if you do it wrong. Use this information, not to draft your own SNT, but rather to interview a lawyer. You'd be surprised at what lawyers don't know.

Eligibility for public (welfare) benefits is determined by income and assets. The most common type of public benefit is SSI. Income is cash received from a steady source, such as social security or investments. Assets are usually broken down into two categories; countable (also called non-exempt in some states) and non-countable (also called exempt).

Countable assets include:

- Cash over $2000
- Stocks, bonds
- IRAs, Keoghs
- CDs
- Single premium deferred annuities
- Treasury notes and bills
- Savings bonds
- Investment property
- Whole life insurance (above a certain amount)
- Vacation homes
- Second vehicles and every other asset not specifically listed as non-countable.

Non-countable assets include:

- A house used as a primary residence (in most states this includes two- and three-family homes)
- An amount of cash (usually $2,000)
- A car
- Personal jewelry
- Household effects

- A pre-paid funeral
- A burial account
  (not to exceed $2,500 in most states)
- Term life insurance policies

Countable assets are used in determining eligibility for government benefits. For example, in most states if your child has more than $2000 he would not qualify for SSI or Medicaid (medical coverage). The child can own non-countable assets such as an automobile without losing eligibility. Therefore your trustee could buy your child a car through the trust. However, even though non-countable assets can be held by the trust, they must be reported to the government. Failure to do so may even be a criminal offense.

Income is any cash flow generated by pensions, investments, employment, etc. If your child receives more than a certain amount of monthly income, it will reduce his SSI benefits and may even disqualify him from Medicaid. The same is true if the income comes from the SNT even if it is not given to your child directly.

How to avoid the pitfalls FIRST UNDERSTAND WHAT countable and non-countable assets are. Make sure that your trustee understands that he may disqualify your child from benefits if the trust makes a gift of a countable asset, such as a savings bond. But if the trustee buys your child a house (houses are non-countable as long as your child uses it as his or her primary residence) eligibility will not be affected.

Second, understand that income from the trust, distributed in the wrong way may also disqualify your child. Here is a brief list of types of payments that will and will not effect benefits. Generally your trustee can make direct payments for:

- Medical care and services
- Home care services
- Payment of medical insurance premiums
- Newspaper and periodical subscriptions
- Education and travel

Generally your trustee cannot make payments for:

- Food
- Shelter
- Clothing

Payment for these necessities either directly or indirectly (through third parties) will temporarily reduce or eliminate your child's benefits. The above is just a partial listing of the requirements.

Clara sets up an SNT for her daughter, Mary, who is mildly retarded. Mary receives SSI and Medicaid. The trust correctly provides that Mary's brother Joel, the trustee, can only supplement public benefits. However, Joel incorrectly buys groceries for his sister out of the trust fund. When Mary's case worker finds out, the entire amount spent on food is deducted from her SSI check.

Joel also pays to have special reading classes for Mary and for a specialist to treat her for severe allergies. This will not cause problems with her SSI because these payments are allowed.

As you can see, the law does not follow any discernable common sense principles. You must seek the advice of a lawyer who specializes in this field and follow it to the letter.

WARNING Rules vary from state to state. Under no circumstance should you try to draft a SNT yourself, even if you get hold of a form. This area of the law is so tricky that one false step can cause irreparable damage.

CHAPTER 9

YOUR FAMILY BUSINESS & MARRIAGE — A TRICKY MIX

There are some 20 million small businesses in this country, a third of them owned by women. Although their owners probably never thought about it, the fortunes of all those businesses are inextricably linked as much to marital vicissitudes as to economic swings. A family business, like a house or a bank account, is a marital asset which can be drastically affected by death and divorce.

All in the family

FAMILY BUSINESSES WHETHER they be pizza parlors or art galleries generally conform to certain structures. Here's a profile of a typical closely-held small company:

- There are only a small number of stockholders.
- There is no ready market for the stock.
- Stockholders actively participate in running the business (it is not just an investment).
- The company rarely pays dividends to its shareholders.
- The chief benefits to owners are salaries, bonuses and retirement plans (more important than the value of the stock).
- The owners derive personal satisfaction from being their own boss.
- Other stockholders are often friends and family members.
- The owners want to pass the business on to the next generation.

These companies are the bedrock of the American economy.

They provide financial security for millions of owners, their spouses, children and other family members. When a married business owner gets a divorce the results can cause financial chaos, drive other shareholders crazy and perhaps even destroy the company.

In any divorce, there are many unpredictable factors that affect the way the court cuts up the pie. Privately held businesses are generally considered a marital asset and subject to division. In equitable distribution states (see Chapter 3), either party can get all or none of a company, or anything in between, at the court's discretion. Not a comforting thought when you're trying to run a business. In community property states, the distribution is more likely to be near 50-50. That means a solo business owner could find himself in equal partnership with an ex whom he now despises. Here are a number of nightmare scenarios that demonstrate how divorce can wreak havoc with a small business.

Scenario #1: Denise and Eddie get a divorce. Eddie owns a health club. He's worked like a dog over the last ten years and the business now owns a million dollars in fancy equipment and real estate. The judge gives Denise 50 percent of the company but she decides she doesn't want to be in business with her ex. The easiest way out for her is to dissolve the company and sell off the assets. Eddie is put out of the business that was his pride and joy.

Scenario #2: The judge awards Eddie 51 percent of the company and his wife gets 49 percent. Eddie keeps control of the day-to-day operations of the business but he can't do the big moves that the business needs in order to grow. For instance, an opportunity requiring substantial financing arises to acquire another gym. Eddie knows it's the deal of a lifetime but the law requires a two-thirds majority of the company's shareholders to vote major decisions, such as a merger or major refinancing. Denise says no. Later, Eddie wants to take out a mortgage to expand the business in the next town. Denise says no. Eddie wants to get Denise off his back but he can't afford to buy her out. He's out of the marriage but trapped in the same old marital wars.

Scenario #3: Let's say Eddie owns the business with his friend Len. Eddie has 51 percent of the stock, Len, 49 percent. The judge gives half of Eddie's stock (25.5 percent) to Denise. Partner Len now goes to Eddie and says, "Hey, pal, you only own half as much of this company as I do, I think you should take half as much salary. And by the way, I want to be president."

Scenario #4: Len is going crazy with the constant interference of Eddie's ex-wife who doesn't like the way they run the business. She regularly drags them into court claiming that they are not upholding their fiduciary duty to protect her investment. Len says to Eddie, "I don't want your ex-wife messing up my business." Eddie answers, "I know, but she won't sell and anyway I can't afford to buy her out."

Scenario #5: Suppose Len (formerly the minority but now the majority shareholder) never liked taking orders from Eddie. He gangs up with Denise and together they control 74.5 percent (more than the two-thirds needed to make major corporate decisions). Eddie's ex-wife and partner take out a huge loan which they can't repay and the business goes under. Eddie loses everything.

Scenario #6: Denise and Len decide to sell the business and Eddie gets his share but the business is gone.

You have now seen six ways the owner of a small business can come to ruin through divorce. When you remarry, plan ahead so that you don't end up in such a scenario.

What to do to avoid disaster in a divorce

THE FIRST AND BEST WAY to protect a business from problems arising in a divorce is to draw up a prenuptial agreement that excludes it and any appreciation in its value from the marital assets. There are a number of other things you can do as well.

Every closely held business should have a stockholders' agreement that places restrictions on transferring stock ownership. This is crucial to assure the survival of the business. The purpose of the agreement is to protect shareholders (one or more) from an involuntary transfer of stock resulting from a divorce, death, disability, guardianship or personal bankruptcy of an owner.

Such an agreement can provide that when one of these triggering events occurs, the company (or the remaining shareholders) has the right to buy the portion of stock involved. The price is determined by a specific formula and paid over a certain period of time. The value of the business might be set at two times earnings or book value or a figure updated yearly at the annual stockholders' meeting. The buy-out is generally favorable to the company, say 10 percent down with the remainder over 5 to 15 years.

In the event of a divorce, the company would have the option, but not the obligation, to buy back the stock. If the court awards stock to the ex-spouse, the company could exercise its option, thereby preventing a possibly hostile outsider from causing problems with the business. The company can also purchase insurance to buy the stock in case of death or disability.

A stockholders' agreement, unlike a prenuptial agreement, is for the benefit of the stockholders, as the name implies, rather than the spouse. These instruments hold up well in divorce situations because they meet one of the main criteria: fairness. Since all stockholders sign the same agreement and situations other than divorce (i.e., death, bankruptcy) can trigger the option to purchase, the agreement doesn't single out the spouse for detrimental treatment.

The agreement can be executed before the marriage of one of the owners or afterwards, since it doesn't require the signature or involvement of anyone but the stockholders.

WARNING If you own a business with someone who is married or getting married, be sure to sit down with him and talk about contingency plans if either one of you gets a divorce. Unless of course, you wouldn't mind waking up one day to find that your partner's ex-wife is running your company.

Your business and the grim reaper

LET'S LOOK AT ANOTHER potential crisis for a small business: the death of a married owner.

Two-thirds of people in this country die without a will. When there is a family business involved, under the law the deceased's heirs could become partners in the business. When that happens the other stockholders may be in for a rough time.

If you die intestate (without a will) the probate court will distribute your estate to your spouse, children or nearest relatives according to your state's formula.

Here's a typical example (but not necessarily representative of your state) of what happens with no will: Let's say the deceased (a man) leaves behind a spouse and children. By statute (state law), one-third of the assets goes to the spouse outright and two-thirds are distributed to the children (or their guardian if they are minors). Even if there is a will, most states give the spouse the right to reject it and claim a statutory share. If there are children, the spouse's minimum share is generally one-third of the estate.

In the absence of a prenuptial agreement, this is the way the estate is distributed: An automatic $25,000 off the top of the company's assets in cash, with the remainder held in trust to generate lifetime income for the widow. The surviving spouse also gets a life interest in one-third of the real estate and other personal property including the stock of the business. The rest goes to the children.

Now let's say the deceased wants to leave his business to his kids from a previous marriage and his bank accounts to his second wife. He puts that in his will. But even a will does not insure that the company won't end up in the hands of someone the owner or owners never intended. When he dies, by law the surviving spouse has the option, usually within six months, of taking what's hers in the will or waiving the will and claiming her statutory share (what she would have gotten under state law if there had been no will). Suppose the business has grown greatly since the deceased made out his will but the bank accounts have not. His widow says, "Hold it! I want my statutory share." What happens to the business and the offspring who were supposed to inherit it? Here's an example to answer that question.

Monica owns a publishing company that she runs with her two daughters, Lisa and Teresa. She wants them to inherit the business when she dies. She marries George. After the wedding, the couple revise their wills. In hers, Monica leaves all the stock in her business to her daughters. George leaves his assets to his children from a former marriage.

Monica and her daughters publish a couple of best sellers and the company grows rapidly. The business is worth a $1 million when Monica dies. George looks at the present value of the business and has little trouble deciding to waive the will in favor of his statutory share. He gets one-third of the stock less the $25,000 cash he receives out of the company's bank account.

George's stock is put in the hands of a trustee whose obligation it is to vote the stock in a way that puts money into George's pocket. The trustee wants the company to pay dividends or give

George some kind of job so he can draw a salary.

You can see already the business is heading for trouble. To make matters worse, Monica's estate owes over $500,000 in death taxes. (Most of this liablity would have been avoided because of the marital deduction if Monica had left her business stock to George rather than to her daughters.)

Monica's estate (of which her daughters are executors) attempts to borrow the money from the company to pay George or have the company redeem (buy back) some of their stock. George says "No." So they decide to have the company borrow the funds from a bank. However, the bank will lend the money only if all the stockholders guarantee the company's note. George refuses. Monica's two daughters may be forced to sell their stock in the company to raise money to pay their mother's estate tax liability.

What can you do to keep your business in the right hands after you die?

AGAIN THE BEST WAY TO avoid the possibility of your business going into the wrong hands is not to allow it to become marital property. A prenuptial agreement (see Chapter 2) can exclude the business and any appreciation in its value from marital assets. Remember that full disclosure is essential if the prenuptial agreement is to hold up. When you exclude it you must define its dollar value using standard valuation techniques.

Estate planners have a number of other ways to keep your business out of harm's way. Here is a brief list of some of the possibilities. Only an expert can tell you which are best in your individual situation.

- Set up a trust to avoid probate and possibly save on taxes by removing some of the value of the business from the estate. In some cases, a Q-TIP trust (see Chapter 13) may work.
- Begin a tax-free gift program to distribute shares of the business in increments of $10,000 per year, per individual, thereby moving it into the proper hands and also avoiding death taxes. If you shift more than $10,000 worth of stock you'll probably generate a tax liability but it might be less than the death taxes.
- Consider a buy-sell agreement with the person you want to get your business — your partner, your offspring, an employee or even a competitor. When you die, he has the right to purchase your shares according to a formula for a certain amount over a period of time.

- Create a family limited partnership or "recapitalize" the family business by issuing common and preferred stock. If properly structured you can save substantially on estate taxes, avoid probate and pass control to your children during your life.

WARNING You could do all the right things to put your business into the right hands when you die and still lose it because your heirs couldn't pay the death taxes. It is crucial that you consult an estate planning specialist to be sure that you have covered all the angles.

CHAPTER 10

GUARDING YOUR SECURITY: THE BASICS OF HEALTH INSURANCE

Remarrying couples, being older with more health problems and greater responsibilities, need to think about health insurance more carefully than first timers. Nothing can catapult you into a financial disaster faster than a serious illness coupled with inadequate health insurance. You can do yourself and your family no greater service than to make sure that you are all protected.

HEALTH INSURANCE IS BECOMING a major concern for more and more people. A major illness or even every day health care costs can quickly wipe out a family's life savings. No insurance or the wrong kind can expose you to bankruptcy so you have every right to be concerned about your future spouse's coverage. Being sure that you both are protected and won't lose coverage should be one of your top priorities. In addition, coverage for your children is important, whether or not you are the custodial parent.

Types of Insurance Coverage

INSURANCE IS A DAUNTING subject. There are hundreds upon hundreds of different plans out there. If you feel overwhelmed by the whole subject, you are not alone. Let's look at some of the various types of insurance available to you.

Individual/family plans

PEOPLE TEND TO USE this kind of coverage between jobs and drop it when they can get coverage through work.

Often the most expensive coverage you can buy, individual/family policies can be tailored to your needs when you apply. Unlike group plans, individual policies let you choose the deductible and co-payment options that suit you. Applicants generally are screened closely to eliminate high risk cases. If you have a preexisting condition you may not be accepted, or the policy may exclude that condition, or you may have to pay a higher premium.

Also, these policies never cover home care or custodial care in a nursing home. People with a history of medical problems need to find policies that don't exclude preexisting conditions and do accept any individual or family. These plans are usually noncancelable. Blue Cross/Blue Shield is the best known of these. BC/BS is basically an open enrollment plan that allows you to choose your own doctors and receive types of treatment that another plan, such as an HMO (see below) might disallow. That's the good news. The bad news is the price tag.

Since you are on your own when purchasing individual coverage you must be cautious about what policy you choose and who your agent is. Some things especially to watch out for:

Arm-twisting sales tactics

SMALL INSURANCE companies sometimes send out a very aggressive sales force working out of their homes for jumbo commissions. If one day they decide they're not doing well on health insurance in your state they may pull out altogether. One way to weed out fly-by-night companies is to call your state insurance commissioner to be sure any plan you are considering is licensed in your state and to find out if there have been complaints filed against the company.

On the other hand, companies that do a lot of other kinds of business besides health insurance, (life, auto,etc.) can't just pull up stakes and leave town. Companies can't arbitrarily cancel your policy but they can cancel a whole block of business. The state insurance commissioner has some leverage over them to make them stick it out. Insurance companies are rated for stability. You can go to the library to look up ratings in several books: Standard and Poor's and A.M. Best are two main rating companies.

WARNING The insurance industry has gone through unstable times lately and thousands of people have wakened to find that their companies have declared bankruptcy leaving them stuck with no insurance and unpaid claims. Your best bet is to buy from a well-established company that has been doing business in your state for a long time.

Rate hikes

NEVER PURCHASE A POLICY that rates you individually. That means that the increase in premiums (and there almost always are increases annually) is based on your claims history and not on the experience of the insurance company's whole block of business. You could be priced right out of your policy if you have one bad year. Ask your agent how increases are determined and if there is any doubt get his answer in writing.

WARNING Never lie or omit information about previous medical conditions hoping to keep rates low or just to be accepted. Doing so could disqualify you if you ever apply for benefits for this condition — or even a related illness.

A little shopping help

SOME HEALTH INSURANCE agents are now using a national proposal system called QuoteSmith to bid on individual and group coverage. Agents pay a yearly subscription fee and with a computer can log into QuoteSmith to produce a spreadsheet containing dozens of health insurance plans. You can call QuoteSmith at 1 800 556-9393 and ask for the name of an agent in your area who is a subscriber to the service. When you call the agent, ask to see the spreadsheet so you can compare policies for yourself.

Health Maintenance Organizations (HMOs) HAVE BECOME increasingly popular in the past few years. People have called this the "department store" method of delivering medical services. HMOs have separate departments for different types of care: pediatrics, internal medicine, maternity, mental health, etc., located in the same facility. There are usually no deductibles or sizable co-payments, just a $3 to $5 charge for an office visit or a prescription.

You must use the HMO's doctors and staff for all medical needs for which services are provided. While you are limited to using doctors within the HMO, you may ask to be reassigned to a different one if you feel you are not receiving proper care. If you develop an illness or condition for which there is no qualified staff doctor or if you need major surgery, most HMOs are now affiliated with hospitals that can provide such services. If you have a medical problem when you are out of state there generally are provisions to cover you.

HMOs often are relatively liberal about preexisting

conditions. Single rate or family rates are generally fixed independently of factors like age, smoking, location, or medical history. You do not have to fill out claim forms when you use services. The cost of these plans for an individual is more for younger people, less for older, but generally around the same as an individual health insurance plan.

HMOs really shine if you are a frequent user of routine medical services. Private plans don't usually cover routine physical exams; HMOs encourage them.

TIP If your HMO does not cover a procedure you need, such as chiropractic services, insist on a referral from your staff doctor. The HMO will then be obliged to pay for it.

Preferred Provider Organization Plans

(PPOs) ARE SIMILAR TO HMOs in that you are restricted to specific doctors; however, they are not under one roof. With this system, you are given a list of independent providers in your area and you can choose whomever you wish. Your choice is much wider than with an HMO because there may be several thousand doctors on the list.

As with HMOs, you do not have to fill out claim forms, a big plus for many people.

WARNING If your ex is paying for any type of insurance coverage as part of your divorce settlement, you may lose your coverage when you remarry.

Group Plans

MOST PEOPLE ARE FAMILIAR with the kind of group insurance that an employer offers as a benefit to employees and their families. Similar plans may also be offered through a union, trade or professional association, such as an association of lawyers. Generally, both employee and employer contribute to paying the premiums making this arrangement less expensive for the employee than comparable individual plans. Depending on the size of the group, these plans generally do not screen applicants as closely as individual policies.

Some of the larger companies offer a "cafeteria plan" which sets a dollar amount for coverage, but you can "spend it" however you want by choosing the specific benefits that meet your needs. Choices can even include additional life insurance, disability, day care coverage or extra vacation days.

Group plan health insurance choices could include an assortment of plans such as an "indemnity" plan (where you are reimbursed for your medical claims) an HMO or PPO, a range of deductibles, or dental coverage. If you have children you may choose to go with an HMO or disability coverage in case you are unable to work. If you are near retirement age, long-term care coverage (if available) may be a good choice for you.

Preexisting conditions and group coverage

WHEN YOU AND YOUR partner are planning your future together, if either of you has a preexisting condition, group coverage may be your best alternative. One or the other may even want to consider a move as drastic as changing to a job that will provide the health coverage you need.

When Earl and Dixie decided to marry, Dixie wanted to quit her job to stay home with her young daughter and Earl's three kids from a previous marriage. Dixie had undergone two cancer surgeries four years before. These were covered by health insurance provided by her employer. But with a preexisting condition, where would she get affordable insurance if she quit her job?

Earl had his own business and a family policy for himself and his kids. When he became engaged to Dixie, he considered shifting to a plan offered by a local small business association. He discovered, however, that even though it was a group plan the premiums were higher than he was paying on his own.

Once they were married, he realized, Dixie's history would be factored into his current plan and his premiums would soar. The family might be priced right out of health insurance.

Earl made a bold choice. After considering all the angles, he decided that the surest course for him to provide for his family was to sell his business and accept a job with a large chain that offered excellent health benefits. As part of a large group, Dixie's history would not be scrutinized and the family would be protected.

One note: Since the group plan is offered by his employer, if Earl ever leaves the company, he will lose his coverage. He could get some protection from the following:

What if I lose my job or get divorced?

COBRA, THE CONSOLIDATED Omnibus Reconciliation Act of 1986, provides a temporary solution to a permanent problem. COBRA was designed to protect employees of larger companies (20 or more workers) and their dependents from losing their group insurance coverage because of such events as leaving a job or being divorced. If you have recently divorced, under COBRA you may, at your own expense, continue your group coverage through your former spouse's employer. However, that protection only applies for up to 36 months after the divorce or legal separation. Beyond that, the employer is free to discontinue coverage and you will need to consider making more permanent arrangements. (The law, however, does not mandate that the employer discontinue coverage so as a practical matter you may be able to negotiate coverage for a longer period.)

Is two too many?

IF BOTH PARTNERS ARE employed, you may find when you remarry that you are covered by two insurance policies. If the employee contribution on both is high you may choose to drop one. However, if your plan pays 80 percent, and your spouse's plan will pick up the remaining 20 percent, you would get full coverage. This is called coordination of benefits. Two may not be too many here. Talk to your personnel office to see how this can be worked out.

WARNING In these times of job insecurity consider keeping both policies in case anything happens to interrupt either partner's employment. To keep expenses down, however, you could raise the deductible on the more expensive policy. The less expensive policy will then be responsible for most of the medical bills.

Military Insurance

MILITARY PERSONNEL and their dependents are covered for medical treatment in government and civilian facilities. CHAMPUS, the Civilian Health And Medical Program of the Uniformed Services, offers continuing coverage for certain categories of former spouses of active or retired military personnel.

Basically it is a group plan with co-payments for services in which the participant pays 20 to 25 percent of the medical bills and CHAMPUS picks up the remainder. There is one very big hole in this coverage, however. CHAMPUS sets a fixed amount that it will pay for any particular procedure. If the cost of a procedure goes over the fixed amount, the individual must pay the entire amount, not just the excess. Does this make sense? NO, but it's the law.

Former spouses will be covered if married to a 20-year-service member for at least 20 years. The years of military service and marriage must overlap by at least 20 years.

All other former spouses may purchase coverage through the Uniformed Services Voluntary Insurance Plan, USVIP. To qualify, enrollment must occur within 90 days of the divorce.

WARNING If you remarry, you lose your coverage. (If the remarriage occurs over age 65, however, you could continue to receive coverage if you were not covered by Medicare.)

Federal Civil Service Health Benefits

A FORMER SPOUSE of a government employee who was enrolled in a government-sponsored plan during the 18 months prior to the divorce may be able to sign up for continued health coverage after the divorce. Application for enrollment must be made within 60 days of the divorce becoming effective and can include the spouse alone or with dependent children under age 22. There's one catch: In order to qualify, the ex-spouse must be designated to receive a portion of the employee's government pension or survivor benefit. Divorce attorneys who understand this fine point are careful to be sure that the ex-spouse is not cut out of the pension in the divorce.

Such is the quirky nature of these matters: If your divorce settlement did not give you a portion of your spouse's annuity or survivor's benefit, you are out of luck in getting insurance. At this point you need to check to see if your lawyer knew about and took care of this matter in a QDRO (see Chapter 12) when your divorce agreement was drawn up.

If you marry a government employee, don't let this happen to you. Put a provision in your prenuptial agreement preserving your interest in pension benefits.

WARNING Enrollment terminates if you remarry before age 55. If you are covered under this system, be sure to get your insurance needs taken care of before you walk down the aisle.

Disability Insurance

SURPRISINGLY, YOU FACE a greater chance of being seriously disabled than you do of dying prematurely. Yet relatively few people think to purchase disability insurance. If your remarriage brings with it a number of small children dependent upon you for support, this type of coverage makes a lot of sense. For example, suppose your new wife has three small children who are not being provided for by their father. She would be in a terrible position if you became seriously ill.

Life Insurance — Who should be the beneficiary?

WHEN YOU REMARRY, you will want to look at your life insurance policy and decide whether you want to change beneficiaries. If your children are minors you'll probably want to be sure they are provided for should you die, whether or not you are the custodial parent. If your ex has custody and you feel comfortable that your children's needs will come first, you may choose to make her the beneficiary. You can later switch the beneficiary designation to your new spouse when your children come of age. Or you may decide to get another policy for your new family and leave the old policy in place.

Another alternative: You can provide for your new spouse after your death but have your children be the ultimate beneficiaries of the policy. You might want to consider establishing a trust as the beneficiary of the policy. The trust can have a number of functions including holding money for your spouse's benefit under the control of a trustee while at the same time making sure that your children get it when your spouse dies. (For more on life insurance trusts see Chapter 12.)

CHAPTER 11

RETIREMENT—THE GOLDEN YEARS?

One of the nicest things to see is an older couple shopping for groceries together or working in the garden side by side or walking arm in arm. When we remarry we hope that our marriage will be like that when we get old. Of course, rosy pictures like this are not possible without financial security. In fact, one of the chief reasons (after love) that women remarry is for security in their old age. Their later years are much more precarious financially than men's. A critical issue facing all couples entering mid-life is what resources will be there at retirement age. Let's look at some of the issues surrounding retirement income for remarried couples.

Social Security Benefits in Subsequent Marriages

ALMOST 40 PERCENT of income received by people age 55 and over comes from Social Security. Obviously, the benefits due you can have a significant effect on your future. Married people can claim Social Security benefits in one of two ways: in their own name if they have been employed and accumulated enough credits, or as dependents, whether or not they ever worked. In the latter case they are usually entitled to 50 percent of their spouse's benefit.

This is of particular importance to women who tend to lag far behind men in Social Security credits earned over their lifetime. There are two main reasons for this discrepancy: one, women's responsibilities for homemaking and childrearing generally cause them to spend less time at a job. And two, women on average, still earn only 65 percent of what men make. Therefore, whether or not they have ever worked outside the home, many women will be entitled to a larger Social Security payment as the spouse of a working man than they would receive for their own labors.

Dependents' Benefits

DEPENDENTS' BENEFITS are often critical for women because it is the husband's benefits that provide the wife's old age security. For the sake of expediency, then, let's look at dependents' benefits from the woman's perspective. Obviously, if the husband earned less than the wife, the same considerations would apply to him.

For married people, dependents' benefits derive from contributions made to the Social Security system by the spouse, and are based on income. You are eligible as a dependent if

- you are 62 or older,
- your marriage lasted for ten years or more, and
- you've been divorced for at least two years.

If you have worked, you also will have accrued benefits in your own name. Even if you are divorced, upon your retirement you have the option of taking the Social Security benefits you earned in your own name OR your dependent's benefit which is half of your ex-spouse's benefit. You can't get both so, obviously, you will choose whichever is higher.

These benefits are available even if your ex has not yet claimed his retirement benefits himself or even if he remarries. More than one wife can claim these benefits. The amount will be less if you have unmarried dependent children under the age of 18 also claiming benefits because your family is allotted a specific amount to be shared by all dependent claimants.

WARNING You lose your dependent's benefit if you remarry.

WARNING A former spouse may be able to garnish Social Security payments when alimony or child support payments fall behind.

Survivors' Benefits
(This section applies when your ex-spouse has died.)

A DIVORCED OR WIDOWED person is entitled to a Social Security survivor's benefit of 100 percent (not 50 percent as with dependents' benefits) of the deceased former spouse's benefit, if their marriage lasted ten years or more.

WARNING If you remarry at age 60 or older, you will continue to qualify for Social Security survivors' benefits from your former spouse regardless of your new spouse's income or assets — even if the person you marry is a millionaire — on ONE condition: **the marriage must not occur within two years** after the death of the former spouse.

Here's an example of unfortunate timing of a remarriage that cost one spouse thousands of dollars.

Christine and Arthur were childhood sweethearts; yet each had married someone else. After Christine's husband Tony died, Christine (age 59 at the time) was faced with serious financial problems. Arthur, now divorced, was her constant companion and support. They were married 23 months after Tony's death. Christine was shocked when a friend told her that she would have been eligible for survivors' benefits from Tony's Social Security had she waited just one more month before getting married. That one month cost her dearly. She would have been entitled to receive benefits of over $1,000 a month for the rest of her life!

The two-year rule holds true even if your former spouse remarries and then dies. In the following case the unfortunate consequence of poor timing befell a man:

Harry was an artist who had earned less Social Security credits than his wife Jeannie, a college administrator. His marriage to Jeannie ended in divorce after more than ten years. After the divorce, Jeannie remarried and several years later she died. Around that time, Harry met and married Bernice, a fellow artist who also had minimal Social Security credits. Soon after, he turned 60 and went to the Social Security office to find out what benefits they were eligible for. He learned sadly that he would have qualified for survivors' benefits through his marriage to Jeannie had he not remarried within two years after her death. Dependents' benefits based on her earnings would have been substantially more than his own or Bernice's benefit.

WARNING You are still entitled to survivors' benefits even if your ex remarries and then dies providing YOU don't remarry within two years.

Survivors' benefits if your spouse dies

IF YOUR PRESENT SPOUSE DIES, you will be entitled to survivors' benefits if you

- are 60 or older, and
- had been married to the deceased for at least nine months.

You can claim the survivor's benefit from either your first or second spouse, whichever is higher, but not both.

Social Security Disability Benefits (This section applies only to people who are disabled.)

SOCIAL SECURITY PROVIDES benefits for people who are disabled because of illness or accidents, work-related or otherwise. In order to collect, you must have a physical or mental impairment that prevents you from doing "substantial gainful work". The disability must have lasted for a period of one year or more.

Special rules that apply to disabled widows or widowers and divorced people may be affected by remarriage. If you are disabled and over 50, even if you do not have enough work credits, you would be eligible for disability benefits through your former spouse as long as

- he/she had enough credits at the time of death or divorce;
- the marriage lasted at least ten years.

Whether you are widowed or divorced, disability benefits, unlike retirement benefits, terminate upon remarriage. There are only two exceptions for whom benefits continue after remarriage: an able widowed spouse over age 60 or a disabled widowed spouse over age 50.

WARNING If you are younger than the cutoff point and really need these benefits to survive, you may want to reconsider getting married. An informal domestic arrangement may be a better idea.

Are there pension benefits in your future?

THERE ARE THOUSANDS OF different private pension plans and each operates under laws and regulations that may affect one type but not another. If either (or both) of you has a pension, now is a good time to scrutinize what kind you have and what you can expect from it. You're never too young to think about how you will be providing for yourself in your retirement years.

Government Pensions

GOVERNMENT (ALSO called "public") pensions cover federal or state employees who have worked for as little as five years and may permit retirement as young as age 55. Unlike Social Security, there are thousands of different plans, so look closely at what benefits are available to widows, widowers and ex-spouses.

Private Pensions — What kind do you have?

COMPANY PENSIONS today provide people age 55 and up with about 17 percent of their income. Approximately half the working population is covered by some kind of company pension plan in which the employee and the employer both contribute a certain amount of money to a fund. When you retire, the fund pays you a certain amount of money. Most pensions fall into one of two groups:

1. Defined Benefit Plans, the most common type of plan, are so-called because a formula, based on how much you made and how long you worked, *defines* exactly what *benefit* you will be paid when you retire.
2. Defined Contribution Plans *define* what is paid in the *contribution*, rather than what is paid out in benefits. The employer pays in a fixed amount based on the worker's salary or the worker's share of the company's profits (called a profit sharing plan). The fund then invests in stocks, bonds or other presumably safe investments. Retirees receive what was paid into the fund plus a percentage of the earnings. What you get depends on how well the fund's investment portfolio performed.

In either type of private pension, what you see may not be quite what you get. Some plans "integrate" your Social Security benefits with those of your pension. What that means is subtraction, not addition, and less money for you. The plan may deduct a portion or all of your Social Security payments from the amount of monthly income they give you.

Either type of plan may pay you a lump sum when you retire or monthly installments for the rest of your life. Some plans also pay a monthly annuity to your spouse if you die within a certain period of time after you retire. This period is generally five to ten years, during which time your spouse will be eligible for a "survivor's annuity". At the end of this period, the annuity ends.

Survivors' benefits

THE RETIREMENT EQUITY ACT of 1984 (REA) requires that all plans that pay annuities offer a joint and survivor annuity. That means in the event the pensioner dies, the survivor automatically receives a lifetime monthly income unless it is waived in writing.

Even pension plans not covered by REA (such as an IRA or some Keoghs) frequently allow the person receiving the pension to choose a survivor election. For example, if you take the survivor benefits election, in addition to receiving an annuity yourself, upon your death your spouse would receive a lifetime annuity too. If not, your spouse might receive nothing other than a lump sum of what you actually paid in (if anything) during your life. In another form of survivor benefit, the pension may only pay out if the pensioner dies within a certain period, typically five or ten years. The survivor is only covered for that period and then the benefit terminates.

If you have this type of pension, there is a trade off to consider. If you elect survivor benefits, your retirement income will be less. If you don't, your spouse may face financial hardship when you die.

In deciding whether or not to elect survivor benefits, you and your spouse should weigh the benefits and disadvantages of each option. If you are over age 60 and you live in a cap state which limits Medicaid eligibility to people receiving a very low income (see Chapter 12) you *must* consider the consequences if you ever need to apply for Medicaid. If your spouse already has substantial independent retirement income, survivor benefits may not be necessary.

In order to evaluate your pension benefits, you will need to see a "summary plan description". Employers are required to give you this short version of your pension plan which will explain your retirement, survivor and disability benefits but probably not mention all the restrictions and loopholes. You can also ask for a copy of the whole pension plan (which may be a beast of 75 pages or more). The pension manager can also provide you with a statement of the current balance in your account.

Pension Points to Ponder

THE WORST SURPRISE A person can face at retirement age is to discover that the pension that was to provide security and peace of mind is not there. For instance:

When Dr. O'Malley died in 1982, his widow was comforted by the fact that he had been paying into a hefty pension plan for many years. Imagine Mrs. O'Malley's dismay when she learned that her husband had assigned the death benefit not to her but to Flo, his secretary and mistress of many years.

This was a true story (names changed to protect, etc.). The Retirement Equity Act largely did away with this kind of bad surprise. It covered all qualified retirement plans including most types of pensions (except IRAs and Keoghs) and established one protection of particular importance to the spouse of the pension holder: The law prohibits him from unilaterally removing his spouse's name as beneficiary (the "anti-alienation rule"). The spouse herself can waive the annuity benefit but only via written consent in front of a notary public or a plan official.

The laws governing pensions are complex but deserving of attention. The REA requires all *qualified retirement plans* to include a *joint and survivor annuity*. That statement requires some definitions: "Qualified retirement plans" include 401(k), stock bonus, defined benefit, money purchase, target benefit, profit sharing plans and ESOPs.

A "joint and survivor annuity" is a lifetime monthly payment for the plan participant and after his death a survivor annuity of at least 50 percent of the monthly amount for the spouse. After (usually) one year of marriage a joint and survivor annuity automatically kicks in. That means that upon her spouse's death, a widow will receive a monthly payment for the rest of her life unless she has waived it in writing. (The same applies for widowers.)

Since many, but not all, plans fall under REA you will want to have your accountant take a look. Profit sharing, employee stock ownership and 401K plans are exempt from the annuity requirement but not the spousal waiver provision. State, federal and military pensions are exempt from both.

WARNING If you are covered by a plan that does not fall under the REA guidelines, you might be left unprotected without your knowledge. For instance, if the plan allows the employee to borrow from the pension fund without your consent the anti-alienation rule may be voided, even if you agreed to the loan. Also, under some plans if the participant's employment terminates he would be able to take his pension out in a lump sum without your consent.

QDROs — Somebody got there first

IF YOU MARRY A PERSON with a pension there may be great benefits waiting there but they may have already been given to someone else. That someone else is most likely an ex-spouse and/or the children from a previous marriage.

More and more, when the pie is divided up in a divorce, pensions are being considered an important marital asset. In some cases, the pension may be worth more than the house. A divorce settlement can include a QDRO (Qualified Domestic Relations Order, pronounced "quadro") which assigns to the former spouse and maybe their kids a portion of the benefits earned during the marriage, to be paid directly into a separate account. Once given away, they cannot be taken back. The subsequent spouse is out of luck unless the previous spouse dies first. In that case, the plan might allow the benefits to go to the next spouse.

WARNING If a QDRO exists, it will not be part of the pension documents. You'll need to check the divorce agreement to find it.

In divorce proceedings, QDROs are negotiated like alimony. Unlike alimony which usually terminates upon remarriage, a

QDRO may continue after remarriage, depending on what was agreed to in the divorce. It's a good idea to check for a QDRO when you get remarried. Here's an example of pension benefits that didn't exist:

When Anne, a widow, married John, a divorcee, they were both in their early sixties. When John died two years later, Anne was shocked to learn that the survivors' benefits in his pension were not available to her because under his divorce agreement he had given them to his ex in a QDRO.

Anne still might get benefits if the ex dies but they will be greatly reduced because of the QDRO. QDROs can also be given to children. If they are, there is little likelihood of ever getting the benefits back through death.

Here's an example of another way you can lose access to a pension:

When Elizabeth, a teacher in her thirties, met Winston, a lawyer, she owned a small house from her first marriage that had appreciated nicely over the years. When they got married she sold it and pocketed $100,000. Winston said that she might consider putting the money into some kind of pension plan to save on taxes and suggested that the money could go into his pension fund (through his personal corporation for his legal practice). She deposited the money in their joint account and he later transferred it to the pension account.

When the marriage failed six years later, Elizabeth wanted her money back and was dismayed to learn that she did not have access to it. Since she was not an employee of the corporation, she could not take money out of the pension fund.

Technically, Winston should not have put her money into his account since the plan was based on employee earnings. He was able to get away with the maneuver by claiming during the divorce proceedings that the money deposited was indeed from his earnings. Elizabeth unfortunately had no way to earmark it as hers.

This is another example of why a little professional advice goes a long way when making decisions about your assets and your future security.

Your pension and your kids

WHAT IF YOU WANT THE money in your pension to go to your children and not your spouse?

Let's say you have a pension plan balance of $500,000 and your children are the beneficiaries when you die. You may be concerned that if the marriage doesn't work out your pension will be in the pot to be divvied up in a divorce. So you plan to deal with that issue in a prenuptial agreement by specifically exempting it as a marital asset.

That takes care of protecting your pension in the case of a *divorce*. But it doesn't cover what happens if you *die*. Once you marry, irrespective of what the prenuptial agreement says, the survivor benefit automatically goes to your new spouse. Your children will be cut out.

WARNING The law in effect places your spouse's name on the pension whether you want it there or not.

Even if your fiancee agrees to waive benefits in the prenuptial agreement the law says that the benefit can be waived only by the *spouse* in writing in front of a notary public or a plan official. Your fiancee is not yet your spouse so the waiver clause of your prenuptial agreement doesn't count. The clause can spell out that your fiancee agrees to sign the waiver once you are married. But practically speaking you'd have a hard time enforcing it. What would you do, go to court and ask a judge to force your spouse to sign? How? You can't send him to jail for refusing! One option might be to diminish other benefits proportionately if the waiver is not executed.

Protecting pension benefits in your prenuptial agreement

IT'S NOT UNUSUAL for couples to have two valuable pensions between them. As long as both continue to work, they don't have to be concerned with who gets what pension benefits in the event of a divorce or death. But in other situations pension benefits do require consideration. One example is when one partner quits work to care for children or a spouse's aging parents. Or, what if a woman marries a much older man who falls ill, requiring her to quit work to care for him?

If you quit your job your pension benefits may be drastically reduced. But your prenuptial agreement can anticipate the consequences to your financial security in the future. In effect, you can ask your lawyer to write into the prenuptial agreement a provision that gives you a sum of money or monthly benefits if certain things happen (i.e., you quit your job, you divorce, your spouse dies).

Be sure you chose an advisor who has experience in dealing with pensions. If something is inadvertently built into or left out of the agreement that is disadvantageous, you might not find out about it until years later. It doesn't hurt to look at these issues early as you plan for your future.

The older the couple, of course, the more germane is the issue of pensions. However, the importance of a pension also grows as the age disparity between the partners increases. Consider this case:

Marianne, a nurse, met Joe when he was in the hospital after suffering his second heart attack. Despite a 19-year difference in their ages, they became close friends and continued seeing each other after Joe was released from the hospital. A year later, they decided to get married. Since Joe was not in good health, Marianne realized she eventually might have to cut back to part-time or even quit her job at the hospital to look after him. She worried about what that would do to her pension. So they drew up a prenuptial agreement that took into account the value of her lost pension benefits and the negative effect on her income of her taking early retirement. A pension actuary was consulted to determine the value of her lost benefits. Marianne hoped for the best but was protected if the worst occurred.

When the pension involved is substantial, it is a good idea to have the lawyer who draws your prenuptial agreement consult with a specialist, such as a pension lawyer (a so-called "ERISA" attorney, after federal laws that govern pensions) or a pension actuary. Pension actuaries are specialists whose credentials may include membership in the American Academy of Actuaries or federal licensing as "enrolled actuaries." These professionals know the fine points of pensions and can catch things that might be overlooked by someone less experienced —small items that can become big problems later.

WARNING Pensions are a complex specialty. Don't try to do it yourself when working out pension benefits in your prenuptial agreement. Get a pension specialist.

CHAPTER 12

AGE 55+ WHAT YOU ESPECIALLY NEED TO KNOW

There are a number of financial issues that apply only to older couples. Some of them are so important to your security that you ignore them at your peril.

AS YOU GET OLDER, HEALTH PROBLEMS become the biggest threat to your financial security. If either partner is near retirement age, you must be aware that if one has a major health problem both will feel the effects financially. Your first consideration should be to make sure you both have good insurance coverage AND an asset protection plan in case of a long-term illness. Many people forget about the latter issue but read on and you will understand its importance. Let's look at your insurance options.

Medicare

MEDICARE IS A PUBLIC health insurance program for people over 65 or people who are disabled. Everyone who paid the minimum into the Social Security system, or who is married to someone who did, is automatically covered. You are entitled to this coverage whether you are rich or poor, in good health or bad. Types of coverage are divided into two parts: Part A covers such things as hospitalization, up to 100 days of skilled nursing home care per illness, and limited home care benefits. There is no monthly charge for Part A but substantial co-payments are required.

Part B is not free. It costs about $30 a month which is deducted from the beneficiary's Social Security check. It pays for such things as physicians' services, outpatient care, lab tests, and medical equipment. There are deductibles ($100 in 1992) and a co-payment of 20 percent that the individual is responsible for.

Neither Part A nor Part B covers long-term care or a nursing home. Another program, Medicaid, pays for that but only after you have exhausted virtually all your assets.

Medigap insurance

PARTS A AND B DO NOT PAY for many routine medical needs like prescriptions, glasses, dental visits, hearing care, or routine exams. To cover the gaps and co-payments, many people buy a supplemental policy known as Medigap insurance.

WARNING This type of insurance never covers long-term care, custodial home care or nursing homes. If you want that kind of coverage, you must specifically choose a long-term care policy.

Until recently, scores of insurance companies promoted hundreds of different Medigap policies that were so confusing that the federal government stepped in with regulations to protect the public. Companies have had to streamline their policies, weed out the worst abuses and limit variations so the consumer can comparison shop more easily.

WARNING Under the new guidelines, insurance companies must offer you Medigap coverage regardless of your physical condition when you are between the ages of 64 ½ and 65 ½. Companies are free to screen out high risk applicants who are older, so if you are not in good health, don't wait. (For help choosing a Medigap policy see Resources, Insurance.)

TIP Medicare sets fixed amounts that it will pay for given procedures. To control fees, some states prohibit doctors from charging more than the Medicare amount and "balance billing" the patient or the patient's insurance company for the difference. Residents of states that do not restrict the practice of balance billing may find a Medicare supplemental policy especially attractive.

If your spouse is on Medicare and you are not

THIS IS ONE OF THE MOST difficult situations that anyone remarrying can face. If the spouse on Medicare is still working, the company is probably paying for a Medicare supplement (Medigap) plan. If your employee group is small and applicants are rated individually, coverage for an older spouse can be extremely expensive and your company may not be willing to pick up the cost. Individual plans are also tied to age and therefore are expensive and limited. If your group is a large one where you won't be individually rated, you may be able to buy insurance through the company if you agree to pick up the cost. Although it will be expensive, it will probably cost less than an individual policy. Or you might find that an HMO would be the most economical. The only way to decide is to shop around and compare.

If the personnel department can't give you the answers you need to work out coverage, ask for the name of the servicing agent (that's the person who gets the commission for the group plan) or call the insurance company directly.

Your best bet is to go right to the supervisor of the department you are dealing with. Many insurance companies work with and understand the complexities of divorces, separations and remarriages. They want your business, so don't be intimidated if it seems that you are getting the runaround.

Except for people who are uninsurable, many situations can be accommodated if you reach the right person.

Long-Term Care Insurance THIS IS THE ONLY FORM of insurance at this time that covers long-term care and nursing homes. Unfortunately, it is very expensive ($1,500 a year and up for a good policy at age 65 — and that only covers one spouse!). Couples over 55 who remarry may want to consider this type of policy for one big reason: A prenuptial agreement will not protect assets in your name if your spouse suffers a catastrophic illness and needs long-term care. Medicaid, the public program that pays for nursing homes, will require both of you to spend down your assets before qualifying for assistance. For people who can afford it, long-term care insurance can bring peace of mind.

WARNING Long-term care insurance is a relatively new product and many policies on the market are not worth the paper they're written on. Before you buy anything, you must go to the library and read the article entitled "The Traps in Long-Term Care Insurance" in the June 1991 issue of Consumer Reports.

There are ways to protect your assets in the event of a medical catastrophe other than purchasing insurance. Here is a crash course.

Protecting assets and income from catastrophic illness and nursing homes

CATASTROPHIC ILLNESS CAN be a double tragedy; not only do you lose your health, you also lose your financial security.

Maye, age 53, married John, age 61. Maye had assets of over $500,000 left to her when her first husband died. John had assets of around $60,000. Maye had children and grandchildren that she wanted to provide for after her death. Because of the discrepancy in their financial situations, they drew up a premarital agreement keeping their assets separate. Eight months after their marriage, John suffered a massive stroke which left him severely debilitated. Maye was unable to care for him and he had to be placed in a nursing home which cost $57,000 a year. Although he was relatively helpless, his health was stable and he could live for many years.

When the home looked at the couple's financial statements, Maye was told that her money as well as John's would have to be used to pay for the nursing home. Maye protested that they had signed a prenuptial agreement keeping their money separate. "Sorry," the officials told her. "Your money is considered joint funds, regardless of your *agreement. All you are allowed to keep is $68,700."* They were right.

The harsh realities THIS IS THE TERRIBLE TRUTH that most people don't learn until it's too late: If one spouse is hit by a catastrophic illness requiring a nursing home, the couple will most likely be wiped out financially. Not even a prenuptial agreement, no matter how carefully drafted, will protect the assets of either spouse. All assets, no matter whose name is on them or who brought them to the marriage, are lumped together and all are considered joint and subject to being spent on a nursing home.

Nursing homes average about $35,000 a year nationally; in urban areas the cost reaches $60,000 a year and up. Long-term care is not covered by Medicare or regular health insurance like Blue Cross/Blue Shield. And, in most cases, the V.A. won't pay.

So who pays? YOU DO! AFTER YOU ARE VIRTUALLY bankrupt, Medicaid, a program designed for the poor, steps in to pick up the bills.

That's the bad news. The good news is that the law allows you to protect yourself, if (and it's a big IF) you know how.

Here's how the system works:

Eligibility for Medicaid is determined by two factors. The first is assets — meaning anything you own that has value. Although that definition may seem simple enough, Medicaid divides assets into three categories: non-countable (also called exempt), countable (non-exempt) and inaccessible.

A non-countable asset can be worth hundreds of thousands of dollars but you are not at risk to lose it and it never disqualifies you from receiving Medicaid.

Typically, non-countable assets include a house (if used as a primary residence), an amount of cash (usually $2,000, for a single person), a car, some jewelry and household effects.

Everything else is countable and would have to be spent to zero before qualifying for assistance. Countable assets include: cash, stocks, bonds, single premium deferred annuities, IRAs, Keoghs, CDs, savings bonds, treasury bills, investment property, whole life insurance (above a certain amount), vacation homes, most investment properties, and second vehicles. In other words, if it's not non-countable, it must be "spent down" to zero.

In most states, a couple's home is protected. However, because of strained state and federal budgets, it has become more difficult or impossible for surviving spouses to protect the house if they are institutionalized.

How to protect assets

TO KEEP FROM BEING driven into poverty by the cost of long-term care you must protect your countable assets. If you ever need long-term care, to get into a good nursing home you should expect to pay your fair share out of pocket. But the goal is to qualify for Medicaid before your financial security is seriously eroded.

The basic strategy is to move your countable assets into the inaccessible category. Here are the ways to do this:

- Give them to a trusted relative, like a son or daughter, to hold for you.
- Set up an irrevocable trust (also called a Medicaid trust) which names someone other than yourself or your spouse as trustee. The trustee is allowed to give you the income but you totally give up your right to get the principal. Why do that? Since you can't get the money, neither can Medicaid. (A revocable trust is no protection because if you can get the assets, Medicaid can too.)
- Purchase a long-term care insurance policy.

All of these choices have drawbacks. The worst: when you give away assets or put them in trust you surrender control. From that time on you will have to go to somebody else to get your money.

Assuming you and your partner are both healthy now, your best options for financial protection are only available if you plan ahead. If you intend to take your assets out of your name to protect them, you cannot wait until one of you becomes ill. Medicaid will disqualify you for assistance until 30 months has passed since you transferred them. That means that you will have to pay the bills out of pocket for two and a half years, enough to bankrupt most people.

Let's go back to the two factors that determine whether you will get assistance from Medicaid. We've just discussed the first, assets. The second is income.

Under federal law, a couple's income, unlike their assets, is not lumped together. The wife's income is hers, the husband's, his. Neither is required to contribute any of his or her income to the cost of the spouse's nursing home.

Let's say you have taken your assets out of your name by giving them to your children or putting them in a trust. You have little left to be spent down. Your spouse needs a nursing home. However, depending on where you live, you may still face dire financial risks. Once assets are below a certain point, many states will provide assistance if the patient's monthly income is less than the nursing home's monthly bill. (The at-home spouse's income is not included in determining eligibility.)

But if you live in certain states you may be unable to get assistance even if you have no assets at all. There's one huge problem with income: About half the states "cap" income in determining Medicaid eligibility, meaning that they deny you assistance if your income is more than a certain amount per month, even though less than the nursing home charges.

Look before you leap

ONE OF THE MAJOR DECISIONS facing older people who remarry is whether to move to another state for a better climate, both meteorological and financial. States like Florida and Nevada are especially appealing because of their lower cost of living and lack of state income tax. If you are ill, however, moving to these two states and many others may have dire consequences.

We're getting married and retiring to Florida

GEORGE AND HARRIET RETIRED to Florida. George had a heart attack which left him severely disabled. He was placed in a nursing home and Medicaid picked up $800 a month of the bill.

Larry and Ann retired to Florida. Larry suffered a heart

attack. Medicaid will not give him any assistance if he needs a nursing home. Ann will be bankrupted by the expense.

Same story; different ending. Why the difference? Because Larry's income is a few dollars a month higher than George's. Does this make sense? No, but it's the law.

Florida is one of 21 states that offers Medicaid eligibility ONLY to people with income of less than $1,266 a month (the amount goes up slightly yearly). If your income is even one dollar more per month, you might never get a dime of help — even if you have no savings to fall back on. In the case above, George's income is under the cap while Larry's is too high.

If you move to a cap state, think twice before you give up official residency in a non-cap state like New York or Massachusetts. To retain residency, you must maintain an address, reside there 183 days a year and continue to pay state taxes, if any. At the present, cap states include: Alabama, Alaska, Arizona, Arkansas, Colorado, Delaware, Florida, Georgia, Idaho, Iowa, Kansas, Louisiana, Mississippi, Nevada, New Jersey, New Mexico, Oklahoma, South Carolina, South Dakota, Tennessee, Wyoming, and West Virginia. Other states may join the list as budgetary pressures force them to limit Medicaid.

WARNING Becoming seriously ill in a cap state could have dire financial consequences. If you are a resident of a cap state and you have friends, family and interests in another state that does not cap income, you may want to consider retiring there.

Protecting your vacation home

MANY PEOPLE OWN VACATION properties that they want to continue to use after remarriage. Unlike your principal residence, a second home is considered a countable asset. If you need a nursing home, Medicaid would require you to sell it and spend down the proceeds before you would qualify for assistance.

The two options for protecting your second house are to either give it away or set it up in an irrevocable trust. Let's dispose of the first option right away: Unless you are absolutely confident that your children will make the property available to you in the future whenever you want it, it's not a good idea.

Using an irrevocable trust can be a terrific idea. Sure, you lose the right to get principal from the trust, but you and your spouse can continue to use and enjoy the property for as long as you live. Your instructions to the trustee can be precise enough to give you most of the benefits of direct ownership.

In addition, the trust can provide that if you die first your spouse can continue to use it until he/she either dies, remarries or enters a nursing home. The property is also protected if you or your spouse gets sued because technically you no longer own it. This kind of trust makes sense in terms of good estate planning too. When you die, the property can go directly to your kids thereby avoiding probate.

WARNING Think twice before transferring ownership of property to your children. No matter how close you are to them, if they get divorced or sued your property could end up in the wrong hands. That can't happen if you use an irrevocable trust.

Protecting your pension

RETIREMENTS PLANS ARE another countable asset that you will want to protect should you need a nursing home. The most common types are Individual Retirement Accounts (IRAs) and employer-based plans ranging from Keoghs to 401(k)s. Whatever type you have, if you have the option of taking it as a lump sum (even though you may have to pay a penalty to get it) Medicaid will consider it a countable asset.

Jack and Ruth remarried, both for the second time. They made it a point to keep their assets separate to avoid problems with their children when one dies. At 64 Jack has the option of taking a lump sum from his 401(k) plan or turning it into an annuity. Ruth has a small IRA worth $26,000. They decide to live in Florida.

One problem: If Jack needs nursing home care he will be forced to liquidate his pension plan and spend it on the nursing home. Let's look at ways to protect that money.

The Law

UNDER SOCIAL SECURITY regulations (20 CFR sec 416) a pension is a countable asset. In the example above Jack's pension would have to be cashed in and combined with his and Ruth's other assets. The same regulation specifically exempts the well spouse's pension plan, meaning Ruth's IRA is excluded from being spent on Jack's care. That's the law, yet, as a matter of common practice many states automatically include a stay-at-home spouse's pension plan as part of the assets that must be spent down.

What's at risk

IT IS CRITICAL THAT YOU understand that a nursing home commitment for one could have a serious impact on both your pensions. Stable and secure income is the key to survival for older couples. Asset appreciation is secondary. For most people the goal is to accumulate and hang on to enough assets to generate the income needed to live on. Your pension is crucial to your financial security. There are two ways to protect it.

How to protect your pension — If YOU may need long-term care

IF YOU NOW LIVE IN A CAP state (or are planning to move to one) it is probably a very bad idea to annuitize your pension. The monthly pension check when combined with your Social Security and other income may put you over the cap. A much better idea: Take your benefits in a lump sum even though it will mean a bigger tax bite up front. The money can then be protected by transferring it to your children or setting it up in an irrevocable trust.

If you are living in a non-cap state (one that will qualify you for Medicaid if your monthly income is less than the monthly nursing home bill) your approach may be different. In the previous example, if Jack and Ruth are living in

Massachusetts (not a cap state) Jack may want to take his pension in the form of an annuity. The advantage is that he would save on taxes by not "lump-summing out" and he would not have to transfer the money to his children or set up an irrevocable trust to protect it.

The disadvantage is that if he is institutionalized most or all of the income from that money (assuming he invests it) would go to the nursing home. If Ruth had substantial income of her own this might be a risk worth taking.

One other option: In some states, the sick spouse can transfer assets to the at-home spouse who immediately buys an annuity. Effectively, an asset which would have gone to the nursing home has been converted to income for the at-home spouse which Medicaid cannot take.

If YOUR SPOUSE were to need nursing home care

AS NOTED, MEDICAID IS NOT supposed to consider a well spouse's pension as a countable asset and demand that it be used to pay for the other's nursing home care. It does happen, however.

Assuming that your state Medicaid office understands the regulation, your best option probably would be to annuitize your pension thereby turning it into a monthly income stream.

By law you have no obligation to contribute your income to the nursing home and it should never be used in determining Medicaid eligibility for your spouse.

Before you make up your mind about how to take your pension benefits, consider whether you and your spouse will want to relocate to a cap state. A decision to annuitize could be a disaster if you move and then need nursing home care.

WARNING The various strategies for protecting assets discussed above require an attorney experienced in elder law. This is a highly specialized field. Your family lawyer may not be the right person to help you with these matters. For more information on the subject, you can order the authors' previous book, HOW TO PROTECT YOUR LIFE SAVINGS FROM CATASTROPHIC ILLNESS AND NURSING HOMES, by calling 1 800 955-2626. If you need a referral for an elder law attorney in your state, see the Lawyer Referral Form at the back of the book.

Moving into a retirement community together

NANCY AND WARREN, BOTH over age 55, planned to be mar-

ried. Each owned a home. They decided to sell their homes before the wedding so they could both take advantage of the one-time-only exemption from capital gains and move to a retirement community.

They signed an agreement with the facility and paid a fee of more than $90,000. Less than two years later, Warren died. Nancy stayed on but within a few months her health declined. She received notice that she had to leave within 30 days. The reason given: "Your physical and mental condition fails to meet the standards set by the Corporation." She had to move in with her daughter who spent the next three years and thousands of dollars in lawyers' fees trying to get the money back. She was only partially successful.

This nightmare is experienced by thousands of older Americans. Enticed by the promised security of a "life care" or "continuing care retirement community" (CCRC), prospective tenants sign a contract and pay an "entrance fee" which buys a life-time residency in the facility. A monthly fee provides for services such as meals, housekeeping, laundry and nursing care, if needed.

Unfortunately, these agreements can be a minefield of problems. Sometimes the facility has the right to terminate the contract on the basis of health and put the occupant out within as little as 30 days. There may be various extra charges in the fine print and clauses allowing the CCRC to hold your money until they resell your unit after they have evicted you. In the last few years, a disturbing number of these facilities have gone bankrupt, leaving their residents homeless.

WARNING An agreement with a Continuing Care Retirement Community (CCRC) is a binding legal contract involving your security and a lot of your hard-earned money. Have it reviewed by your lawyer or financial advisor. You both might profit from reading the "ABA Checklist for Analyzing CCRC Contracts" available from the Commission on Legal Problems of the Elderly, 1800 M Street, N.W., Washington, D.C. 20036.

Of course, not all of these facilities are bad. If you are considering a CCRC, check to see if it is accredited by the industry's self-regulatory body. (See Resources, Senior Issues)

Who will make decisions for you if you become incapacitated?

MARIA SUFFERS FROM CHRONIC asthma. One day she has a severe attack and is rushed to the hospital. The doctors revive her but lack of oxygen has caused severe brain damage. Marie is on life sup-

port systems. Her husband says that Marie would never want to go on living in a vegetative state. Her children from a previous marriage want everything possible done to keep her alive, whatever her condition.

Under the stress of the situation her husband and children are in a horrible battle. Her husband says it is cruel and dehumanizing to keep her alive when she would have hated being like that. Her children say they will never give up hope and that their stepfather is more concerned with paying for her care than preserving her life.

Who has the power to make decisions about whether to continue life support, Marie's husband or her children?

Neither. The only person who can make this decision is Marie herself. Unfortunately, she is now unable to make her wishes known.

This issue concerns all adults but becomes more important as you grow older. What kinds of life-sustaining measures are acceptable to you? Tubal feeding and hydration? Respiratory support? Would you want your heart re-started if there were no chance that you could return to normal cognitive functioning? Whom would you entrust with the power to carry out your wishes should you be unable to speak for yourself?

A health care proxy, also called an advance medical directive, deals with these issues. This legal document can relieve your spouse and other relatives of a terrible burden and give you the peace of mind of knowing that you will be able to die with dignity.

In it you can designate a person to act as your proxy to implement your wishes. It is your decision whether it will be your child, your spouse or someone else. Your only criteria should be that you have discussed your wishes with this person and have confidence that he or she will carry them out. Don't rely only on the document alone; there is no substitute for sitting down with your family and your doctor and making your wishes clear.

Each state has it's own regulations concerning these directives. For more information see Resources, Senior Issues.

Power of attorney — regular, durable and "springing"

A POWER OF ATTORNEY is a legal instrument that gives to another or others the right to handle financial affairs such as writing checks or selling stock. The person given this responsibility does not have to be an attorney. Many people give a power of attorney to a spouse so that if anything were to happen to them, their spouse could manage the family finances.

A **regular power of attorney** does not have an expiration date but ceases if you become incapacitated. A **durable power of attorney** is the same except that it does remain valid if you become incapacitated. It can be an effective tool in planning to protect assets if a spouse needs a nursing home. Both of these become effective at the time you sign the instrument. In some states you may put two people (your spouse and your daughter, for example) on the power of attorney so there are checks and balances. Another option: A **"springing"** power of attorney that becomes valid only if/when you are incapacitated.

WARNING Giving a power of attorney is giving away control. It is not advisable to do this unless it is absolutely necessary. It is better to give it to someone trustworthy to hold until it is needed with instructions about how and when it will be used.

WARNING A power of attorney can become "stale". The biggest mistake lawyers and financial advisors make when recommending a power of attorney is to forget to inform their clients that most financial institutions will not accept them after a period of time. There is no set policy on how long that may be. However, a power of attorney is only as good as an institution's willingness to accept it. Update yours at least every two years, if only by changing the effective date.

What if there are two houses? Tax problems!

IT'S NOT UNUSUAL FOR each half of a couple to own a home. Couples sometimes want to hold on to both houses with the idea that they may let their kids use one or rent it or just make up their minds about the second house later after they settle down. From a tax perspective, there is a serious question about whether both homes should be brought into the marriage. Couples with one or both partners approaching or over the age of 55 should take particular note. Here's an example to show you the kind of problem two homes can cause:

Estelle and Bob are getting married. Both are over 55 and both own homes. After their marriage they decide to live in Bob's house and sell Estelle's. Estelle will lose the once-in-a-lifetime tax exemption on the first $125,000 in capital gains on her home because only a primary residence qualifies for the exemption and they are living in Bob's house.

On the other hand, what if Estelle sold her house prior to the wedding? Assuming she had been living in it (it must be her principal residence to qualify), she would keep her capital gain exemption. But not if she sold it the day after her wedding. Why? Because a couple is allowed only one exemption for one *principal* residence. The entire gain on the sale of the second house would be subject to taxation.

WARNING If you are planning to sell two primary residences and move into a new home together after you are married, be sure to sell both properties before you say, "I do." That way you will both be able to claim your $125,000 capital gain exemption.

CHAPTER 13

AFTER YOU'RE GONE: ESTATE PLANNING

When you remarry, there are a number of issues involving estate planning that you will want to discuss with your new spouse and probably other family members. Most people have given some thought to whom they want to have their assets when they die — their spouse, their children or others. And most people also put off doing anything assuming they will get around to it someday. If you're getting remarried, "someday" is here.

What is estate planning?

WHETHER YOU HAVE just a tidy nest egg or major assets like property, investments or a successful business, the biggest risk to your "wealth" is the huge tax bite that Uncle Sam takes out of your estate when you die. If your estate is worth over $600,000, you will pay death taxes of anywhere from 37 percent to 55 percent. And that's just federal tax. If you live in a state that has a death tax, the figure could go much higher. Don't forget there could be complications in probating your estate with, of course, attendant legal fees. By the time your money gets to your heirs there could be very little left.

An estate planning specialist can help you put together a program that removes all or most of your estate from probate, eliminates or reduces the tax bite, and provides funds to pay whatever taxes can't be avoided. Beyond a will, most of the beneficial effects will likely be accomplished by more sophisticated tools such as trusts. Let's look at some of the ways you can set up your estate.

How to pass assets to your heirs

THE SIMPLEST WAY TO PASS along assets is to **hold them jointly** with the person you want to get them when you die. Assets held jointly automatically belong to the survivor.

Another way to distribute assets is ***through a will***. A will is simply a set of instructions spelling out who gets what. This document only applies to assets held in your name alone which require a process called probate to transfer them to new owners. Your will tells the probate court what you want to have done. The court has the responsibility to carry out your wishes.

If you die ***without a will*** (intestate) no one knows what your wishes were so the probate court steps in and directs where the assets go according to a formula. You have forfeited the right to have a say in the matter; state law decides for you. Your spouse gets a "statutory share", generally one-third (or as much as one-half), with the balance going to your children.

There's one big problem with probate: It is a public process where everyone knows your financial business and your relatives can go to court to fight over your money. Probate can be contentious, lengthy and expensive with attorneys' fees taking a big bite. That's why one of the first objectives of estate planning is to avoid probate. Let's look at some of the painful scenes you can avoid with good estate planning.

When bad things happen to people who don't plan

MONROE, A WIDOWER, marries Marlene, a much younger woman, after a whirlwind courtship. Monroe's grown children, Ann and Tim, are surprised that their father is acting like a kid but pleased that he seems to have a new lease on life.

Pertinent facts: Marlene has a daughter, Tracey. Monroe has a house worth $200,000 and cash and investments of $500,000.

Marlene and Monroe's children do not like each other. Monroe is aware of the animosity. He wants to be sure Marlene is provided for after his death but have Tim and Anne to get what's left when she dies. A few years after the marriage, Monroe dies of a heart attack.

Scenario #1: Monroe dies with all his money and his house jointly held with Marlene. Because the assets are held jointly, they automatically go to Marlene.

Tim and Anne file a lawsuit claiming that their dad never intended for Marlene to get all his assets; that her name was on them for convenience in case he became ill. Weighing in their favor is the relatively short duration of the marriage. They also contend that their dad had not been thinking clearly and that Marlene was putting pressure on him when he put her name on his assets. Will Marlene win? Maybe, but she'll spend a fortune in legal fees.

Scenario #2: Monroe has a will which provides that Marlene inherits $100,000 and the balance goes to Anne and Tim. Marlene has the legal right to waive the will and take her statutory share. By the laws in their state she can get $233,100 instead of $100,000 as Monroe had intended. The only good news here is that legal fees will probably be minimal because Tim and Anne can't fight it. Unfortunately, Monroe's wishes are thwarted.

Scenario #3: Monroe has a will that gives everything to Marlene. Tim and Anne can file a lawsuit and argue that the will is void because their dad was mentally ill or unduly influenced by Marlene.

Sounds crazy? Unlike the criminal justice system where you are presumed innocent until proven otherwise, in the bizarre world of probate and civil matters you are presumed guilty and therefore must spend thousands of dollars on lawyers to defend yourself.

Will the will be upheld? It almost doesn't matter because the battle will be so bloody and expensive.

Scenario #4: Monroe dies without a will. Marlene will end up with a share based on the formula provided by laws in the state where they reside, generally about one-third. The balance goes to Tim and Anne. Good news: No one can fight it. Bad news: The estate goes through probate eating up time and money, and Monroe's wishes will never be known.

What got lost in all these scenarios is that Monroe really never gets his wish to provide for Marlene and upon her death make sure his assets go to his children. In fact the only thing he accomplished was to make sure that everyone will be unhappy and that some of his money will probably go to lawyers, Marlenes's daughter or her next husband!

What's the best way to provide for your spouse but make sure that your kids get their share?

ONE OF THE BEST WAYS to do this is to set up a trust to hold your assets. A trust is a legal instrument established by one or more people to hold assets. It is set up for someone's benefit (the beneficiary) and it is controlled by a person called a trustee. When you set up a trust, it becomes the owner of the assets, not you. Assets not in your name when you die are not part of your estate and do not go through the probate process. That's one big plus. Another attractive feature of trusts is their ability to give you maximum control of where your money goes after you die.

A trust is an especially useful tool in remarriage when you want to provide for your spouse after you die but make sure your money ultimately goes to your children, not your spouse's children or her next husband. Used along with a prenuptial agreement, it eliminates or greatly reduces the possibility of a challenge by your spouse or other heirs, cuts legal bills and avoids scrutiny by the court.

If you want to avoid the sort of problems that confronted Marlene and Monroe, consider setting up a trust. But not just any sort of trust. You need one that is unfamiliar to many people, even to many lawyers and financial planners: a Q-TIP trust.

This comfortable acronym stands for Qualified Terminable Interest Property trust. A Q-TIP trust has a number of attractive features:

It allows your estate to avoid probate and puts your money in the pockets of the people you want to have it. Moreover, it can

- provide financial security for your new spouse but not his/her kids;
- protect your spouse from your kids;
- protect your kids from your spouse and his/her children; and
- save a bundle in federal and state death taxes and legal fees.

A Q-TIP operates according to a specific set of rules. Here's how it works:

As we've seen, in each state, a surviving spouse is entitled by law to a specific percentage of the deceased spouse's estate (generally one-third if there are children or one-half if there are none). This is called the "statutory spousal share". The survivor will automatically receive this amount in the absence of a will. If there is a will giving her less than that amount, she has the right to disregard it and claim her full statutory share.

Now let's go back to our example to see how a Q-TIP would help Monroe and his family. Monroe, you may recall, has a problem. He wants to provide for Marlene after he dies but make sure that what's left of his money goes to his children after her death. Here's how he does it:

Step 1: Monroe and Marlene draw up a prenuptial agreement (see Chapter 2). All the rules about these agreements — full disclosure, fairness, no undue pressure, and representation on both sides — are important at this time. He asks her to waive her statutory rights in consideration of their marriage. Marlene agrees to waive her rights to an automatic percentage if he makes provisions for her care after his death.

Monroe and Marlene get married. (By the way, once the waiver has been signed, if Monroe drops dead the day after the wedding, his estate will go to his children not to her.)

Step 2: Monroe sets up a Q-TIP trust. He names his wife as the beneficiary and his accountant and good friend, Ed, as the trustee. He puts into the trust $500,000 in CDs paying five percent interest. The trust specifies that after his death, his wife gets all of the income from the money ($25,000 a year) during her lifetime, and that upon her death the principal goes directly to Anne and Tim.

But, Monroe wants to do more for his wife. He puts in a provision called the "five-five power" which specifies that every year Marlene may take out of the principal in the trust up to $5,000 or five percent whichever is greater. In this case five percent, e.g., $25,000 the first year, is what she could take out. Moreover, in case of emergencies or other specific situations, Ed, the trustee, has discretion to give her more of the principal. After her death, whatever money is left, net of taxes and undistributed income, goes directly to Tim and Anne. Marlene's child, Tracey, has no right to claim any money in the trust.

A Q-TIP is a trust revocable by Monroe while he is alive. Monroe can be the trustee and receive the income and principal. It becomes irrevocable only when he dies. Since it is revocable, Monroe technically can change the terms, but if he does he breaches the prenuptial agreement.

Tax benefits

THERE'S A BIG TAX advantage to a Q-TIP trust: Monroe is

able to take advantage of something called the "marital deduction". Current estate tax laws allow one spouse to leave unlimited assets to the survivor without incurring a death tax. Ordinarily in order to avoid a tax, Monroe would have had to leave the money to Marlene outright. But if the Q-TIP trust is set up properly, his estate gets the marital deduction even though Marlene is getting only the income generated by the money for her lifetime and a piece of the principal.

Death taxes won't be due until after Marlene dies, when Tim and Anne inherit the balance. Marlene's estate will owe death taxes, but that's not fair to Tracey who is expecting to inherit her mother's money. The trust, however, contains a provision that Marlene's estate will be reimbursed before the funds are distributed to Monroe's children. That means Tracey doesn't end up paying taxes on Tim and Anne's inheritance.

If after several years of happy marriage, Monroe wants to leave Marlene more of the principal (not just the income), he can do so. In fact the premarital agreement can specify that she will get a certain percentage of the principal, (commonly five percent but any amount is allowed) for each year the marriage lasts up to, say, 50 percent, and that whatever is left at the time Monroe dies will go to his children.

Advantages to Marlene

MARLENE MAY FEEL uncomfortable that the trust becomes irrevocable at Monroe's death. After all she cannot change its terms. But there's good news too. Not allowed under the Q-TIP rules: Monroe cannot specify that Marlene will forfeit the money if she remarries. The money is hers till she dies.

If the trust and prenuptial agreements are properly drafted and executed it is very difficult for anyone to break them. That means Marlene can't be sued by Tim and Anne. Financial security and perhaps family harmony are maintained.

When husband and wife can't agree on how much she is to inherit

LET'S SAY MARLENE IS uncomfortable about waiving her statutory share because the state they live in gives a surviving spouse one-third of the deceased's estate. Monroe's estate is worth $700,000. Marlene therefore is giving up $233,333 in cash in exchange for a yearly income of $25,000 and the option for an additional $25,000 in principal per year.

Does that mean Monroe can't set up a Q-TIP? No, he could state in his will that his wife is to get her statutory share and then do a Q-TIP for whatever remaining portion he chooses to put aside to generate income for her. Monroe may be upset, however, because he would like to have more go to his children. That's why these matters must be discussed and settled before the marriage and made part of the prenuptial agreement.

Maximum benefits from life insurance

Q-TIP TRUSTS ARE A GOOD way of dealing with substantial assets. But what if you don't have a big estate? Here's another way to accomplish the same thing:

Let's say Monroe hasn't got a lot of money so he wants to "create" an estate for his wife and children by buying life insurance. Monroe is in good enough health that life insurance premiums are affordable. Again he wants to provide for his wife first but make sure that the money goes to his children when she dies. He can set up a life insurance trust with the trust as the owner of the policy and reap almost the same benefits as with a Q-TIP trust. Here's how:

The life insurance trust buys a policy on Monroe's life that pays the trust $500,000 upon his death. (Monroe could also assign an existing life insurance policy to the trust.) The trust provides that Marlene will receive all income and a certain amount of principal per year. If properly drafted, insurance proceeds in the trust avoid taxes at Monroe's death and are excluded from Marlene's estate when she dies *thereby avoiding estate taxes completely. The instrument is irrevocable once the terms are set so Marlene's interests are protected as well as the ultimate heirs', Monroe's kids.*

In the above discussion, there are a number of tax considerations which are beyond the scope of this book. Whenever there are significant assets involved, or even if there are not, the money spent on a specialist in estate planning is an investment in your peace of mind and the security of your spouse and children.

You will need a sophisticated professional to take full advantage of the tax code. Unless your needs are very simple, your family lawyer may not be the best person to help you. If you need assistance in finding a tax and estate planning specialist, see the Lawyer Referral Form at the back of the book.

Protecting family land

ONE OF THE MOST OVERLOOKED areas of estate planning is family land. Like any other asset, it can be affected disastrously by a divorce or the death of a spouse. Here's a case in point:

Nancy inherits a beautiful piece of property, a 500-acre tract of land in North Carolina. Her family has enjoyed the property for years, fishing and boating on the lake and spending summers in the cottage built by her grandfather. She hopes her grown children and grandchildren will continue to enjoy it for many more years. Nancy marries Dan who also has grown children.

Scenario #1: Nancy and Dan's marriage does not last. The marital assets are split and Dan gets half the property. His sentimental attachment to the land is less than Nancy's so when a big developer makes him an offer, he sells. The developer puts in a road and scores of tract houses. The constant traffic, speedboats on the lake, and recreational vehicles in the woods destroy the wilderness-like quality Nancy loves. Her share is greatly devalued.

Scenario #2: Nancy dies intestate (without a will). The property is divided between her husband and her children. Her children sell off a big parcel to pay the death taxes. The property continues to appreciate in value. When Dan dies years later, his children from a previous marriage inherit his share of the property. There are huge estate taxes due again. Nancy's children want to preserve the land, Dan's children want to sell it. A bitter battle ensues. The land is cut up and sold.

How to shortcircuit disaster

TO ELIMINATE PROBLEMS in the event of a divorce, Nancy excludes the property from the marital assets in a prenuptial agreement. She then executes a "conservation easement" to preserve the land for her children and future generations. Here's how:

Nancy calls in a lawyer and a land-use planner. Together they draw up a conservation easement (a recorded restriction on the property) allowing only limited development on the land. She decides that she will permit the cutting of timber and farming to generate money to pay the taxes. The land-use planner helps her choose a portion of the property which could be divided into lots and sold if there is a need to raise money in the future. The areas selected could be used without harming the beauty and usefulness of the remaining parcel. Nancy donates the easement to a land trust (a charitable conservation organization) and takes a big tax deduction. The family still owns the land but now its use is restricted.

When Nancy dies, there's less of a tax bite because the value of the land is greatly diminished: The easement would prevent a big developer from buying it thereby keeping the value down. And the land is protected because it can never be developed beyond the minimal areas allowed in the easement. Without these measures the land certainly would have been lost.

(For more information on protecting family land, see Resources, Books.)

CHAPTER 14

WHAT'S WRONG WITH THE SYSTEM? WHAT ISN'T!

I doubt if there is one married person on earth who can be objective about divorce. It is always a threat, admittedly or not, and such a dire threat that it is almost a dirty word.

— Nora Johnson

LOOK AT IT THIS WAY: Who in his right mind would board an airplane that had a 50-50 chance of crashing? Yet those are the odds millions of us accept when we say "I do." For those whose marriages crash, the consequences are horrendous: In a study asking people to list the most painful experiences of their lives, divorce placed at the top of the list.

When a marriage ends, husband, wife and children are catapulted into the legal system where their futures are determined by forces largely beyond their control. More than a million American families a year undergo this ordeal.

These families are part of the bedrock of our society. It is critical, then, that there be an effective system to help them through the most difficult life transition with a minimum of financial disruption and emotional pain. So how well is our system doing? Is it effective? Are the reforms of the past two decades working?

Failing grades

HERE'S HOW THE SYSTEM worked for two couples in different circumstances and different states:

- A successful young doctor in California marries his secretary. The marriage lasts three years; there are no children. The ex-wife, age 27, receives a divorce settlement of half a million dollars over the following three years.

- A couple in Texas are married for 29 years with three children. The husband is a successful engineer, the wife, a full-time homemaker. In their divorce, the wife receives no alimony and loses her health insurance. She uses her $60,000 settlement to live on and looks for a job. With no work experience she can only earn the minimum wage. In four years she will be broke and 60 years old.

What kind of marks do you give a divorce system that permits this kind of "fairness"?

Law implies consistency. So where is it?

THE LAWS IN THIS country are so varied and their application so inconsistent that divorce attorneys will expend great effort and extravagant amounts of their clients' money maneuvering to have their cases heard by one judge rather than another and even in one state instead of another. But no matter where they go, the process will not be smooth.

Our legal system everywhere is collapsing. Family courts are overburdened, understaffed, underfunded. There are not enough judges to handle the enormous influx of problems — family violence, juvenile delinquency, sexual abuse — associated with our troubled times. Most judges have had no special training in divorce issues and rule according to their own set of biases and experiences.

Even the best judges with the best of intentions don't have time to give each divorce careful scrutiny. The most the system can do is to move the divorce along so that the court can deal with other more critical matters — a battered woman who needs a restraining order because she fears for her life, a nine year old boy accused of selling heroin. With cases like these awaiting attention, courts can barely squeeze in "normal" families undergoing a divorce.

Pushing a divorce through the courts today may take from one to six years and cost thousands of dollars. It's not uncommon for middle class couples to each spend $10,000 or more on legal fees — money that comes out of funds intended for braces or camp or college for the children. Here's what the price tag was for one family:

- A middle class couple in New Jersey divorce after 16 years of marriage and two children. The battle is lengthy and ugly on both sides. Ten years later there

> is still so much bitterness in the air that the parents cannot even make plans for the children's visitations without a court-appointed psychologist overseeing the arrangements. For this the wife spent $41,000 on her lawyers, the husband, $27,000 on his.

What kind of marks do you give a divorce system that costs so much? Yet there seems to be no way to contain costs. When Massachusetts did away with fee guidelines on the grounds that they constituted price-fixing, clients had no idea what a divorce should cost and for many, fees went through the roof.

Divorce is unfair to men. MANY MEN GET HIT with grossly unfair divorce settlements particularly in states that automatically divide the marital pie down the middle, as in the case of the doctor above. But a blow to the wallet may not be the worst of it. Millions of men lose out on one of life's most rewarding and precious experiences, that of raising their children.

In 90 percent of today's divorces, the wife is given physical custody of the children. Even if the father wants to keep them, his work and living circumstances often make it unfeasible. So he pays child support and sees his children every other weekend and on some holidays. But he has lost forever the opportunity for the intimate daily relationship that develops in an intact family.

If he remarries, he must hope that his new wife has financial resources of her own. For most divorced fathers, the burden of paying the bills for two households limits or precludes the possibility of more children. Many men must content themselves with raising another man's children with their second wife.

Divorce is unfair to women.

WHEN MOTHERS HAVE custody of children the problems of being both breadwinner and solo parent are enormous. Child support rarely covers the needs of the children. And few women are able to earn what their former husbands could. They can't change the most intractable wage statistic of the last 30 years: Women still earn only 65 percent of what men make.

The courts generally overlook this fact. The law assumes that both divorced partners are capable of economic independence. Where children are involved, or older homemakers with little or no job experience, it simply can't happen. Over the past two decades this unrealistic economic perspective has driven millions of single-parent households headed by women into poverty. Every married woman's secret nightmare (even upper middle class women) is that her marriage will fail and she will find herself broke and on the street.

Divorce is a disaster for children.

WHEN PARENTS SPLIT up, the children's world collapses into chaos. Children feel terror, loneliness, guilt that they were somehow to blame for the divorce, rejection, conflicting anger and loyalty toward both parents. Studies have shown that the emotional scars often last a lifetime.

The trauma for youngsters is heightened by the fact that divorce is carried out in the adversarial arena of the legal system where they become pawns. The father's lawyer may be coaching him to demand custody as a bargaining chip to lower the mother's monetary expectations or to contest support to "starve her out." The mother may respond by wrangling over visitation and poisoning the children's minds with her grievances against their father.

After the divorce, the children may find themselves alone much of the time. Mom may have to take a job just when they most need her. The child support awarded by the court probably will be inadequate to cover their needs. For a family of four, one-third of the husband's income goes to support three-fourths of what used to be his family. And even at that, half of all children receive only part of the support ordered by the court or none at all. Divorce can mean real economic deprivation for children.

The business of divorce

DIVORCE IS A STATE-OPERATED business that affects more than three-quarters of all Americans, directly or indirectly. Our families are coming unglued at an unprecedented rate fueling a multibillion dollar divorce industry.

Since divorce is a business there must be a profit. Employed in the industry are hundreds of thousands of attorneys; the system is designed so that you have to use them when you get a divorce, whether you want to or not. There are solo practitioners who do a few divorces along with assorted bankruptcies, incorporations and wills. And there are big-name divorce specialists, known to their brothers as "bombers", who employ "scorched earth tactics" against their clients' spouses. With half of all marriages ending in divorce, lawyers share the enviable position that undertakers occupy: They are sure to have a steady supply of customers.

A short history lesson: Divorce American-style

TWENTY-SOME YEARS ago California passed the first no-fault divorce law in the nation. It was hailed as the beginning of a revolution that would bring "fairness" to the process of divorce. It banished a set of divorce laws that were based on the concept of blame and consequences. In the old model, both partners played by the rules or paid the consequences. If the husband, for instance, was caught fooling around, there was a big monetary price to pay in the divorce. But without a "fault" to blame on his wife, a husband could not get a divorce unless she agreed to it. To get her to let go, he had to offer an attractive financial arrangement, in effect to buy his way out. This kind of wrangling and blaming caused no end of psychological and financial damage. But it also meant that if you played by the rules the system would protect you.

With the new laws came the revolutionary idea of marriage as an economic partnership. Should it end, the theory goes, each partner is entitled to a fair (meaning more or less equal) share of the assets, irrespective of who was "right" or "wrong".

Over the past two decades, every state has passed its own variation of no-fault divorce. A few states adopted a version in which the marital pie was cut down the middle and each spouse got precisely half. Most states rejected this strict interpretation and allowed the presiding judge to make the final determination of how the pie should be divided. This is known as "equitable distribution". Alimony was pretty much abolished as too punitive; in its place came two or three years of "rehabilitative support" and then the divorced spouse was assumed to be capable of financial independence. The intent of the law was admirable but its execution has caused at least as many problems as it solved.

Reforms that backfired

EQUITABLE DISTRIBUTION looks great on paper. But while it's been a most uncertain blessing for divorcing couples, it's produced a windfall for their lawyers. The concept of "equitable" is so vague and subjective that lawyers have a field day racking up billable hours dickering over what's "fair." Making matters worse, the whole process is carried on in an inefficient, time-wasting legal system where lawyers have no financial incentive to arrive at a settlement before their clients' money runs out. In truth the new laws in many ways favor lawyers at the expense of their clients.

Family life itself, that safest, most traditional, most approved of female choices, is not a sanctuary: It is, perpetually, a dangerous place.

— Margaret Drabble

TODAY, MARRIED WOMEN who pass up careers to care for children and home face almost insurmountable problems should the marriage end or their husband die. Even if they were once comfortably middle class, without job skills they risk spending the rest of their lives as part of the army of "working poor". In throwing away the concept of alimony the legal system undermined the traditional female role of wife and mother. What kind of marks do you give a divorce system that penalizes women for choosing to be mothers and homemakers?

Divorce by chain saw

AFTER YEARS OF MARRIAGE, couples are bound together by their very nerve endings; their ganglia are intertwined. When divorce is proposed, the first thing both parties do is call a lawyer. Throughout this book you have been urged to consult a lawyer to help you put your financial affairs in order. Now let's look at the dark side of the profession.

A lawyer is the product of a law school. With few exceptions these institutions train students in the techniques of adversarial confrontation. Anything that's legal is fair in the name of winning.

Standard weapons in the divorce lawyer's arsenal: Counsel a husband to stall support payments while the lawyer maneuvers to run up the wife's legal bills. Then accuse her of being an unfit mother to coerce her into a settlement. The wife's lawyer will accuse the husband of hiding money and demand cartons of documents in discovery — every bill, bank statement and check stub he owns.

Never mind that the children will do without necessities because of these vengeful tactics, or that their lives will be torn apart by the rage between the parents that they love. The lawyers will cut the husband and wife apart with a chain saw causing massive bleeding and unbearable pain.

Law schools teach divorce this way. They rarely offer courses in the psychological problems surrounding divorce, or in divorce mediation and negotiation, or in family counseling. Lawyers' training does not equip them to deal with their suffering clients with compassion, patience and a healing approach. It's just luck if you find one whose character supplies the qualities that his schooling deemed unimportant.

It gets worse: Shady ethics

A 1992 REPORT BY the New York City Department of Consumer Affairs examining the way divorce lawyers do business found widespread illegal, unethical and unfair practices. It uncovered lawyers who padded their bills, demanded large sums of money just before the trial, threatened to walk out, and withheld files so that their client could not switch to another lawyer.

Having rung up big bills, some lawyers resorted to strong-arm collection practices including placing lien's on their client's homes and attaching their wages and bank accounts. Clients who are emotionally debilitated by the agony of a divorce are in no position to defend themselves from their supposed champions. With friends like these, who needs enemies?

...and worse: Lawyers who have sex with their clients

DIVORCE IS AN EMOTIONAL trauma of the worst sort. A woman in the throes of the experience is terribly vulnerable. She sees in her lawyer her one hope for salvation; she trusts him to rescue her from catastrophe. To him she pours out the most intimate details of her life — how much money she has, how much she may get, whether her husband abused her, details about infidelities, her worst fears and deepest pains.

There is a great disequality of power in the attorney/client relationship in a divorce case, much like that which occurs between a therapist and a patient. Yet only a handful of state bar associations frown on lawyers sleeping with their clients while a case is in progress. Disciplinary measures such as disbarment are virtually unheard of, let alone damage awards. The matter's been called the legal profession's "dirty little secret".

One psychologist who works for the probate court in Boston ran a support group for women whose divorces had been particularly lengthy and acrimonious. "As I listened to them," she says, "I was amazed at how many had had an affair with their lawyer. The aftermath for them — and their children as well — was very bad. Their self-esteem plummeted." A call to the state bar association to learn the official position on lawyer/client sex produced this response: "It's not a problem."

Not a problem for whom?

WOULD IT BE A PROBLEM if the powerful professional receiving payment to help these women was their psychotherapist or their physician? Would it be a problem if the lawyer waived his fee in exchange for sexual favors? But it wouldn't be a problem if he continued to bill for his services while enjoying sexual perks? As

N.Y. Times columnist David Margolick notes, "The state of Indiana bars plumbers from engaging 'in lewd or immoral conduct' while on house calls. But the lawyer-legislators who drafted that statute have not applied that same standard to themselves. Indeed, what is sauce for doctors, psychotherapists and at least some pipefitters is not necessarily sauce for lawyers — in Indianapolis or anywhere else." What kind of marks do you give a divorce system that tolerates this kind of abuse?

In August, 1992, The American Bar Association's Committee on Ethics and Professional Responsibility issued a formal opinion acknowledging the "existence and seriousness of problems in this area," and advocating that lawyers refrain from sexual contact with clients. However, the opinion has no teeth. It does not impose an absolute ban on sexual contact as does the medical profession's, nor does it apply any sanctions such as disbarment or even suspension of the lawyer's license to practice. Moreover, it is not binding in any jurisdiction.

Any solutions?

AS LONG AS WE VIEW divorce as a conflict between two economic competitors abetted by their legal gladiators it will continue to be a tragedy for American families. Lives will continue to be damaged, children will be wounded and already scarce resources will end up in the pockets of lawyers instead of on the backs and in the bellies of the children. So long as the system is fundamentally adversarial it cannot be reformed.

Divorce is a painful transition for all members of the family. Matrimonial Lawyers must be trained to assist gently in that passage. Law schools must add courses in palliative skills such as mediation, psychotherapy and grief counseling. A plumber is required to have a license to put in a bath tub; lawyers who handle divorces should be required to be certified as capable too.

Better yet, most divorces should be taken out of the courts entirely. A major goal should be to get divorce away from the lawyers and into the hands of social workers and mediators whose skills lie in healing, repairing and resolving conflicts rather than fueling them. Divorce could largely be handled administratively rather than legally in much the same way that we handle licensing.

Myth versus reality

"AMERICANS, WHO make more of marrying for love than any other people, also break up more of their marriages, but the figure reflects not so much the failure of love as the determination of people not to live without it." That's the quote that began this book. But is it reasonable to expect that we can go from marriage to marriage seeking total fulfillment with the "right" partner? Margaret Mead saw another side of our nature: "People often cling in their minds to a pattern far removed from the realities of everyday life," she observed.

The truth is most of us can't afford divorce. In 1969, seventy percent of households were married couples; by 1989, only 56 percent were. Divorce, separation and failure to remarry has had a disastrous effect on family income, pushed middle class families below the poverty line, and accounted for many of the economic problems we've faced in the past twenty years.

The bottom line: Money

SEVEN OUT OF TEN MARRIED couples with children have two working spouses supporting one household. Two salaries barely cover one family's expenses. Two separate families cannot live as cheaply as one. Where is the money to come from to support two households, let alone more children in subsequent marriages? In the best of times, judges have few options to provide adequately for the children of divorce. In economic hard times, there is simply not enough to go around.

There are no easy answers or painless solutions. Everything we do in life has consequences. We are clinging to unrealistic expectations about marriage and divorce that cost us untold pain and billions of dollars in wasted legal wars. We face the death of an illusion as unrealistic in today's world as the notion of recreational sex in the age of AIDS. This is the truth: Only the rich can afford sequential monogamy. For Elizabeth Taylor it's fine; for the rest of us it doesn't work.

Taking your marriage into your own hands

REMARRIAGE WITHOUT financial risk, the title of this book, is virtually an oxymoron. Once we get entangled there are always risks. Does that mean, then, that we should not marry?

No, not at all. Human beings need love, commitment, predictability, safety, companionship, routine, comfort and a place to come home to. The family provides all this through systems and structure in which parents and children can grow and thrive.

If you have already been through a divorce, you know that when your systems broke down, strangers took over to provide a system for you: lawyers, judges, accountants, psychologists, social workers, guardians ad litem, strangers who handled your family and your problems as a business.

The point is not that we should forego marriage but

that when we marry we must do so with a greater sense of personal responsibility. If we don't act with more forethought and caution, we again will be forced to turn our lives over to strangers.

In Chapter 2 we said we would not try to convince you that you need a prenuptial agreement. By the time you got to the end of this book, you'd understand their benefits. You are at the end. What you should understand by now is that a prenuptial agreement is a system that you design yourself at a time when you are in your right mind. You and the person you love set up a structure, a framework in which to conduct your marriage and, fully as important, to dismantle it should that undesired possibility ever arise. Now, before you get married, is the time to use lawyers to draw up your agreement. If you ever find that you need to get unmarried you won't need them.

Conclusion

THE IDEAL DIVORCE revolution would make getting married harder to do, make getting divorced easier, and make having children hardest of all. For it is the children who are the innocent victims of our illusions about marriage and divorce. We have no business bringing children into a world of broken homes. We cannot accept another 14 percent drop in two-parent families and a tripling of the number of divorces — a repeat of what we witnessed in the past two decades.

If we as parents and husbands and wives do not empower ourselves to take our lives into our own hands, if we do not wake up to reality and act responsibly, we will create a generation that does not know how to build a family and we will endanger, perhaps to extinction, the very bedrock of society, the family.

We must place a higher value on working out problems before a marriage. The time to find out if they can't be worked out is before the wedding, not after.

CHAPTER 15

RESOURCES

Books on the Issues

■ Second Chances

Men, Women & Children a Decade after Divorce — Who wins, who loses and why

Judith S. Wallerstein & Sandra Blakeslee

Ticknor & Fields 1989

The long-term effects of divorce on children are a shock.

■ The Divorce Revolution

The Unexpected Social and Economic Consequences for Women and Children in America

Lenore J. Weitzman

The Free Press 1985

Required reading for anybody concerned about the problems of divorce American-style. An eye-opener.

Books on Divorce

Why books on divorce? Because you need much the same information preparing a prenuptial agreement as in a divorce. The following two titles cover all the basics in easy-to-understand form.

■ Divorce & Money

Everything you need to know about dividing property

Violet Woodhouse and Victoria Felton-Collins with M.C. Blakeman

Nolo Press 1992

■ The Divorce Decisions Workbook

Margorie L. Engel and Diana D. Gould

McGraw-Hill, Inc. 1992

Additional Copies

■ Remarriage Without Financial Risk
To order additional copies call 1-800-568-5353 or send $19.95 plus $4.00 shipping and handling to:
Financial Planning Institute
P.O. Box 135
Boston, MA 02258
Massachusetts residents add $1.00 for sales tax. New York residents add the appropriate tax in accordance with your area.

Children & Money

■ Administration for Children and Families, Office of Child Support Enforcement
370 L'Enfant Promenade, SW
Washington, D.C. 20447
(202) 401-9373
Offers help in locating missing parents who owe child support. They can provide you with employment and income information of those parents who are neglecting their financial responsibilities and help you work with the child support office in your area.

■ Association for Children for Enforcement and Support (ACES)
723 Philips Avenue, Suite J
Toledo, OH 43612
(800) 537-7072
Offers assistance to parents who are trying to collect child support. You can obtain social security and credit report information.

■ National Child Support Enforcement Association
Hall of States
400 No. Capitol Street, NW, Suite 372
Washington, D.C. 20001
(202) 624-8180
Conducts conferences, seminars and other educational services for professionals in the field of child support. A directory is available for professionals who are seeking information in their respective state.

Credit Reports

If you are denied credit and need to obtain a copy of your credit report, you can contact the reporting agency. For most of these agencies, the first copy is usually free but for additional copies there may be a charge of $5.00 or more.

Three of the biggest credit agencies are:

- Equifax
  Office of Consumer Affairs
  P.O. Box 740241
  Atlanta, GA 30375-0241
  (800) 685-1111
  (404) 888-3500

- TransUnion Corporation
  25249 County Club Blvd.
  North Olmstead, OH 44070
  (800) 521-4019

- TRW
  National Consumer Relations Center
  P.O. Box 749029
  Dallas, TX 75374
  (214) 235-1200

Credit Help

- BankCard Holders of America
  560 Herndon Parkway
  Suite 120
  Herndon, VA 22070
  (800) 638-6407

A non-profit organization that educates consumers about credit. Offers brochures, newsletters and more.

- National Foundation for Consumer Credit, Inc.
  8611 2nd Avenue
  Suite 100
  Silver Spring, MD 20910
  (301) 589-5600

Provides counseling services and information for families in financial distress. For a directory of offices in your state, call 1-800-388-CCCS.

- **Fresh Start!** *Surviving money troubles, Rebuilding your credit, Recovering before or after bankruptcy*
  John Ventura
  Dearborn Financial Publishing, Inc. 1992
  1-800-621-9621 ext. 650

A helpful book on cleaning up your act, credit-wise.

Secured Cards

The following three banks offer secured credit cards. Consult the credit department of each for more information on their services. There may be others in your area.

- First State Bank
  P.O. Box 15414
  Wilmington, DE 19850-5414
  (800) 262-3610

- Home Trust Savings and Loan
  700 22nd Avenue, South
  Brooking, SD 57006
  (605) 692-9555

- Key Federal Savings Bank
  P.O. Box 6057
  Havre de Grace, MD 21078-9978
  (301) 939-4840

Estate Planning

- **Winning the Wealth Game**
How to Keep Your Money in Your Family
  Andrew D. Westhem &
  Donald Jay Korn
  Dearborn Financial Publishing, Inc. 1992

A comprehensive introduction to many of the tools in estate planner's bag of techniques.

The following two titles give the lay person clear information on living trusts and their many uses.

- **The Living Trust Handbook**
  Attorney David E. Miller
  The David E. Miller Law Corporation 1991

- **Understanding Living Trusts**
How to Avoid Probate, Save Taxes and more
  Vickie and Jim Schumacher
  Schumacher and Company
  1990

■ **Preserving Family Land**
Essential Tax Strategies for the Landowner
Attorney Stephen J.Small
P.O. Box 4508
Boston, MA 02101-4508
Send $8.95 plus $2.00 postage and handling.
Make check payable to:
Landowner Planning Center
Available in January 1993

Senior Issues

■ American Association of Homes for the Aging (AAHA)
901 East Street, NW
Suite 500
Washington, D.C. 20004
(202) 783-2242
Offers free brochures on issues relating to quality housing, accreditation health and communities for the elderly.

■ **How to Protect Your Life Savings from Catastrophic Illness and Nursing Homes**
Harley Gordon
with Jane Daniel.
Financial Planning Institute, Inc. 1991
To order, call 1-800-955-2626 or send $19.95 plus $4.00 shipping and handling to:
Financial Planning Institute
P.O. Box 135
Boston, MA 02258
Massachusetts residents add $1.00 for sales tax. New York residents add the appropriate tax in accordance with your area.
Allow 2-3 weeks for delivery.

Medical Directives

■ Over 40 states now have statutes that require a specific form for a living will. For a free copy of the official living will form for your state and guidelines for its use, send a self-addressed stamped envelope to:
The Society for the Right to Die
200 Varick Street
New York, NY 10014
(212) 366-5540

Medical Directives (continued)

■ Doctors Linda and Ezekiel Emmanuel, husband and wife physicians affliated with Massachusetts General Hospital, have designed a comprehensive document that helps clarify what measures you would allow in a variety of different illness scenarios. Called a "Medical Directive," it outlines your values and preferences and deals with naming a proxy and communicating with your doctor.
Write to:
Medical Directive
Harvard Health Letter
PO Box 380
Boston, MA 02117
Send $5.00 for minimum order of two copies.

Lawyers

■ The American Bar Association has been looking at the problem of lawyer/client sex. If you believe your lawyer may have acted inappropriately, write to:
Joanne Patula
ABA Center for Professional Responsibility
541 North Fairbanks
14th Floor
Chicago, IL 60611

Lawyers (continued)

■ **The American Academy of Matrimonial Lawyers** encourages a dignified and humane approach to marriage issues. The 1,200 members have adopted a strict code of ethics. Activities of the Academy include: certification, continuing legal education, examinations written and oral, the Academy journal, arbitration, public affairs and referrals. For information on referrals in your state, call (312) 263-6477 or write to:
American Academy of Matrimonial Lawyers
National Headquarters
150 North Michigan Avenue
Suite 2040
Chicago, IL 60601

■ An eye-opening view of divorce lawyers and their outrageous pratices by the commissioner of the New York City Department of Consumer Affairs, Mark Green: *Picking the Pockets of Divorcing Women*, Lears magazine, September 1992. Go to the library and read it and then write to your congressman and demand reforms.

Insurance

■ **The Medicare and Medigap Update**
For a copy, send a self-addressed stamped envelope and 52¢ for postage to:
United Seniors Health Cooperative
1331 H Street
Washington, D.C. 20005

■ For a reprint of the June 1991 Consumer Reports article entitled **The Traps in Long-Term Care Insurance**, send $3.00 to:
Consumer Reports/Reprints
101 Truman Avenue
Yonkers, NY 10703-1057

■ **Long-Term Care: A Dollar and Sense Guide**
A short but thorough look at the pros and cons of long-term care insurance. Helps answer the question, Is nursing home insurance a good idea for me? 72 pages, $8.50 plus $1.50 for postage and handling.
United Seniors Health Cooperative
1331 H Street, Suite 500
Washington, D.C. 20005
(202) 393-6222

Looking for updated information on Medigap policies? AARP offers two sources:
■ **Medigap Changes in Law and How They Affect You**
(D14509)
and
■ **Medigap: Medicare Supplement Insurance, A Consumer's Guide** (D14042).
To order, include the title and number of the desired publication and write to:
AARP Fulfillment (EE0291)
P.O. Box 22796
Long Beach, CA 90801-5796

The Health Care Financing Administration (HCFA) also offers a publication on Medicare insurance:
■ **Guide to Health Insurance for People With Medicare.**
To order, call
1-800-638-6833.

INCOME-PRODUCING ASSETS

Current Assets	Current Value	Annual Income	How Held			Distribution		
			His	Hers	Joint	His	Hers	Date Recd
Checking accounts - min. bal. kept for no-charge checking								
Savings accounts								
Credit union accounts								
Share draft accounts								
Money market funds								
Certificates of deposit								
Savings bonds								
Promissory notes receivable								
Mortgages receivable								
Rental Income								
Restricted access								
Stock options								
Trust funds								
IRA/Keogh/pension								
401K								
Simplified Employee Pensions (SEPs)								
Legacies								
Residual rights								
Stocks								
Bonds								
Mutual funds								
Syndication interests								

NON-INCOME-PRODUCING ASSETS

Current Assets	Current Value	Annual Income	How Held			Distribution		
			His	Hers	Joint	His	Hers	Date Recd
Personal residence								
Recreational property								
Automobiles								
Recreational vehicles/boats								
Cash value of life insurance								
Business interests								
Home furnishings								
Jewelry/furs								
Antiques/fine arts								
Hobby collection								
Stamp collections								
Foreign currency								
Other								

LIABILITIES

Current Bills Outstanding

Liabilities	Who incurred Debt?	When?	PAYMENTS			
			Monthly Payment	Last Pmt. Made	Final Pmt. Due(date)	Balance Due
Mortgage or rent						
Home-equity balloon loan						
Monthly utilities						
Homeowner's or renter's insurance						
Car insurance						
Life insurance						
Medical insurance						
Charge accounts						
Credit card accounts						
Doctors						
Dentists						
Attorneys						
Accountants						
Subtotal						

LIABILITIES

Taxes to Date Which Have Not Been Withheld/Paid

Liabilities	Who incurred Debt?	When?	PAYMENTS			
			Monthly Payment	Last Pmt. Made	Final Pmt. Due(date)	Balance Due
Federal income taxes						
State and city income taxes						
Social Security tax						
Real estate taxes						
Personal property taxes						
Assessments (sewer,etc.)						
Unpaid income taxes for prior years						
Income tax interest or penalties						
Capital-gains tax						
Subtotal						

LIABILITIES

Loans to be Repaid

Liabilities	Who incurred Debt?	When?	PAYMENTS			
			Monthly Payment	Last Pmt. Made	Final Pmt. Due(date)	Balance Due
Mortgage(s) on home(s)						
Mortgage(s) on other property(ies)						
Car payment						
Car payment (2d car)						
Recreational vehicle payment						
Furniture installment						
Appliance installment						
Home improvement						
Education and training						
Life insurance						
Stock purchase on margin						
Other bank loans						
Debts to friends						
Debts to business assoc.						
Debts due to gambling, drug, or alcohol abuse						
Loans from family						
Subtotal						

LIABILITIES

Contractual Obligations

Liabilities	Who Incurred Debt?	When?	PAYMENTS			
			Monthly Payment	Last Pmt. Made	Final Pmt. Due(date)	Balance Due
Any financial obligations to spouse of former marriage						
Lease Commitments (cars, buildings, office equipment, etc.)						
Medical/dental						
Sales contracts (encyclopedia companies, dinnerware, record & book clubs, enrichment programs, etc.)						
Union and other dues						
Liens payable						
Cosigned loans						
Subtotal						

Contingent Liabilities

(Money you may have to pay if you lose a lawsuit or purchase property that you have already agreed to buy, etc.)						

GENERIC FINANCIAL STATEMENT

Assets

	Indv.	Joint	If joint w/whom
Cash on hand and in banks			
US government securities			
Listed securities			
Unlisted securities			
Mortgages owned			
Accounts and notes receivable due from relatives and friends			
Accounts and notes receivable due from others - good			
- doubtful			
Real estate owned			
Cash value life insurance			
Automobiles			
Personal property			
Other assets - itemize			
Total Assets			

GENERIC FINANCIAL STATEMENT

Liabilities

	Indv.	Joint	If joint w/whom
Notes payable to banks - secured			
- unsecured			
Notes payable to relatives			
Notes payable to others			
Accounts and bills due			
Accrued interest, etc.			
Taxes unpaid or accrued			
Mortgages payable on real estate			
Chattel mortgages and other liens payable			
Other debts - itemize			
Total Liabilities			
Net Worth			
Total Liabilities & Net Worth			

GENERIC FINANCIAL STATEMENT

Source of Income

	Indv.	Joint	If joint w/whom
Salary			
Bonds and commissions			
Dividends and bond interest			
Real estate income			
Other income - itemize			
Total			

Contingent Liabilities

	Indv.	Joint	If joint w/whom
As endorser or co-maker			
On leases or contracts			
Legal claims			
Taxes not shown above:			
Income taxes			
Delinquent or contested taxes			
Other Special Debts			

You may cut out this form or photocopy it (both sides) and then fill it out.

Request for Referral

Please send one or more names and addresses of attorneys in my state whom I can call for help with estate planning and elder law.

We are sorry that we cannot provide referrals for the following states: Alabama, Delaware, Hawaii, Kentucky, Mississippi, Montana, Nebraska, North Dakota, New Hampshire, New Mexico, Tennessee, South Dakota, Vermont, West Virginia, Wyoming, and Washington D.C.

NAME

NUMBER AND STREET

CITY/TOWN

STATE ZIP ( ) PHONE

I have questions regarding:

❑ Estate planning, including wills and trusts

❑ Medicaid planning

Mail to:

Financial Planning Institute
PO Box 135
Boston, MA 02258

Please enclose $12.00 to cover research, postage and handling.

Continued next page

Please read the following carefully:

This service is offered to provide additional resources to readers of this book. Neither the publisher nor the authors receive any referral fee or other compensation of any nature from the attorneys whose names are given out. Reasonable steps have been taken to assure that the lawyers whose names are provided through this service are experienced in the area of estate planning and elder law.

No warranty, expressed or implied, is made as to their competency.

We will try to give you names close to your address, however this may not always be possible.

Please read and sign:

I agree to take reasonable steps to verify the competency of any attorney I engage.

By signing this letter, I release Financial Planning Institute, Inc., and the authors of this book from any liability that might arise from this referral.

______________________________________ __________________

SIGNED DATE

(Referrals cannot be processed without your signature.)

Please allow up to two weeks for a response.

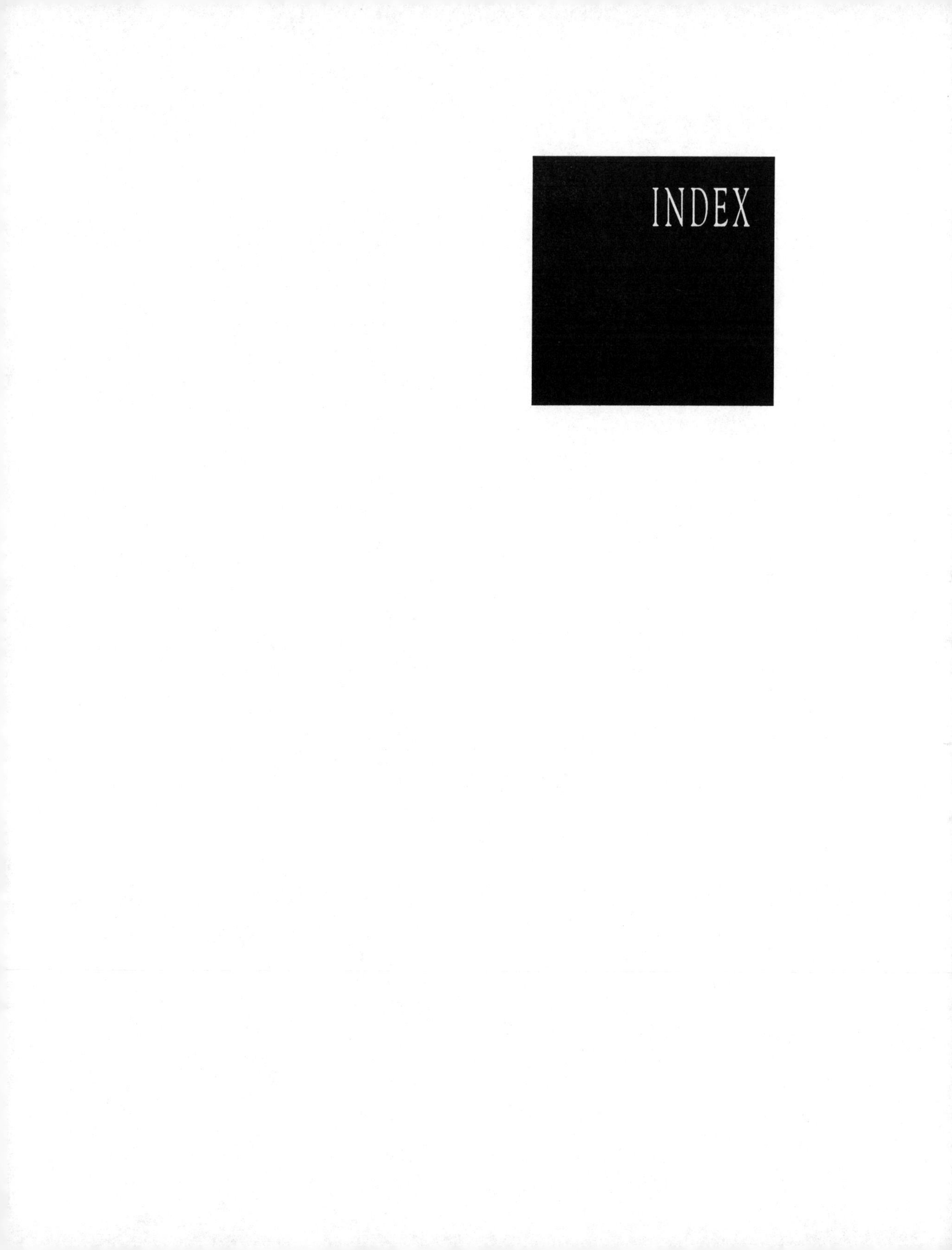

INDEX

POSTSCRIPT

MOST OF THE ANECDOTES *and case histories in this book are drawn from real life but names, occupations and other identifying features were changed to protect the identity of the parties involved. Many depict examples of unexpected things that can go wrong when people marry.*

If you have an interesting or unusual tale to tell in this vein – or a "horror story" – the publisher would appreciate hearing from you. Please write to:

FPI
P.O. Box 135
Boston, MA 02258